When life doesn't make sense, focus on

Seeing Jesus

Jesus in 20/20, Volume 1

Daniel J. Koren

Koren Creations, LLC
Missouri, USA

To

Jesus

who opened my eyes

CONTENTS

WHEN NOTHING MAKES SENSE

Introduction

HAVE YOU LIVED THROUGH those moments where nothing made sense? When life had not gone as planned? Perhaps you were searching for God but it felt He was playing hard to catch.

I've faced dark times in life. A smile on my face with a frown in my heart. You've been there, too.

So had Cleo.

Cleo's whole world caved in around him. Everything he had worked for, prayed for, and focused on came crashing down into a meaningless mess. Tears. Anger. Blame. Questions.

It was all there:

Lies.

Abuse.

Government cover-ups.

Such a maddening twist of fate.

Cleo was not alone in his grief and shock. His wife Mary was reeling, too. She had witnessed the murder first-hand, up close. This husband and wife decided to walk away from it all.

"We just need some space," she said, trying to forget the bloody scene as they walked together.

Sometimes that is all you can do when you can't make sense of things. Stepping back can give you perspective.

It was a crisp, spring day. The honey-butter scents of the almond tree blossoms lured in bees that hummed as they gathered the nectar. If the birds were singing, the two on foot were not listening. They didn't even hear the footsteps of another person out for a stroll as he approached them.

"Mind if I accompany you?" he asked.

Cleo shrugged. "I am not sure we are good company, but yeah, you're good."

"What are you discussing? You both look so sad!"

Cleo replied, "You must be the only person staying in Jerusalem who hasn't heard about the things that happened this weekend!"

"What things?" the newcomer asked.

Cleopas explained, "The things about Jesus from Nazareth!" He began to describe the story to the unknown traveler. The religious leaders had plotted His murder. And succeeded.

"We were all hoping that Jesus was the one who would set Israel free from oppression. It is all so real, though. For three years we knew Jesus and talked with him almost every day. Now, for three days, we have been trying to handle life without him."

"Tell him about this morning," Mary prodded, knowing it was not polite for a Jewish woman to speak to a man she did not know.

Cleo obliged her. "Some of the women, who are his followers like us, say they saw angels who told them Jesus is alive. A couple of our guys checked out the scene at the tomb and found it empty. They didn't see Jesus."

Now sad himself, the traveler looked at them and sighed. He muttered, "So thick-skulled and slow to believe!" He began to explain how and why the Anointed One had to suffer those things. Using the Scriptures by the prophets and Moses, he explained it all.

After two hours of walking and talking, their heads and hearts had grown full but their bellies, empty. "We have reached our destination," Cleo explained, pointing to the little village. "This is Emmaus."

"Well, it was nice visiting with you," the traveler said.

"Please, won't you come in and eat with us?" the man invited. "You can stay here for the night and continue tomorrow when you have had a good rest. We enjoyed hearing what you had to say."

The stranger accepted the invite. Later, they let him do the honors of speaking the blessing and breaking the loaf of bread for the meal. He had done this often with them. Cleo's and Mary's eyes opened. At that moment, they saw Jesus.

Mary exclaimed, "Jesus!"

Cleopas gasped.

Jesus disappeared.

That couple had been looking at and talking with Jesus for a long time, but something supernatural happened when they began to eat. Like the travelers[1] on the road to Emmaus, you and I have let misunderstandings blind us from Jesus. Tragedies and disappointments leave us looking but not seeing.

Jesus is right in the middle of your mess. You might not see Him[2] yet. You may have glimpsed Him a little. When He opens your eyes, you never see anything the same again.

Yes, this book is about seeing Jesus. You might know a little bit about Jesus or a whole lot. Either way, there is much more to see. Those folks had spent years with Him and still did not "see" Him.

As the two travelers demonstrated, physical eyes cannot "see" Him. We need spiritual vision to see Jesus because often He is right with us and we do not notice. Their spiritual eyes saw Him just before He disappeared. They continued "seeing" Him even after their physical eyes couldn't because their hearts had opened.

Is Jesus alive in your life? Or are you questioning Him? Blaming Him? I've done it. As I write this, my family and I are walking a less-traveled path, needing His insights daily.

You also want to see Jesus better; that is why you are reading this. Would you be willing to walk away from everything

---

[1] See this story in Luke 24:13-31. While Luke does not name the second traveler, it appears John does. In John 19:25, we learn that Mary, the wife of Clopas (a variant spelling from Cleopas) was at the scene when Jesus died on the cross. It would make sense then that they travel home together and discuss these events on the way. However, this account does not focus on the identity of the second traveler, but on the One to whom their eyes were blinded.
[2] In a stylistic choice, I have capitalized pronouns and nouns referring to Jesus Christ. In keeping with the purpose of this book, this helps us think of Him in exalted terms, not just common.

for a while? Let's stroll through the Gospels. As we walk together, He will open our understanding.

It's funny how you and I ended up on the same path. I'm not sure which side road got you here, but I would like to hear about it. You can find me on the main channels of social media and I would love to hear from you. As I'm able, I respond to emails, direct messages, and other forms of communication I receive. So please, drop a note and introduce yourself!

Let me share where I am coming from. I'm tired of hearing success speeches and motivational talks in churches. It feels like someone has plundered the Bible for techniques and strategies rather than letting it do its work on us. Often, churches try to mix Jesus and the world system in a custom blend: hipster Christianity, shabby chic religion, a spiritual combination as appealing as organic broccoli blenderized with instant pudding, or a clash of alfalfa sprouts with an energy drink.

I'm not bitter about religion but I'm concerned about the direction the broad swath of believers is going. If you ask the person on the street what Christianity is about, you will hear something about music, preachers, lights, scandals, political views, musty buildings, bake sales, or some program a church did in the community. The world sees a lot of Churchianity. They should see Jesus.

The church world today wants market appeal but lacks clarity on what it is supposed to be. So they mix lattes and Living Word. Often they do a good job of neither. They hide Jesus and blind themselves by reaching for a trendy ideal that isn't worth attaining and accomplishes nothing of His desires for us.

I love church—the one Jesus began. We can recapture what that should be. He will show us how.

The two travelers on that road of life commented afterward how Jesus kindled a fire within them. Their hearts were burning as He opened up the Scriptures to them. Do you want the Bible to speak to you and rekindle your spirit? Do you want to grasp God's plans for you? You will as you get closer to Jesus and see Him.

More than anything we must see Jesus. Something has hidden Him from our view in some way. It could be sinful choices, moral wounds, or religious tradition. Many who claim to know Jesus cannot see Him like those two committed followers of His could not see Him.

I am talking about more than having a vision. You could have heard the clap of His sandals, have seen His robe snapping in the winds of Galilee, and have looked into His penetrating eyes, yet you might not have "seen" Him. Judas did, as did many others.

Some have encountered the resurrected Jesus and later let that moment fade. With time they went back into godless lives. We want more than super-sensational experiences.

In contrast, this book is about a different kind of seeing Jesus. To be "seeing" Jesus means your spirit will perceive Him in a new way. You will own this relationship, not a mass-marketed salvation experience at a religious gathering.

Once you see Him as He desires you to, everything will make sense. He is the light and seeing Him helps you see everything else in right perspective. Welcome to a paradigm shift. This new way of thinking will refocus your friendships, your occupation, your home-life, your hobbies, your finances, and even your words and thoughts. If you are not ready to be reformatted, you might close this book now and slowly back away.

You have come too far and been through too much to give up now. Your battles, scars, barriers, and terrors are not enough to stop you. Jesus comes alongside to give meaning to your journey and finish it with you.

On the other side of seeing, you will not be able to stop yourself from telling others about Him. Cleo and Mary ran back to the hiding disciples who had not yet seen Jesus and told them everything. As they opened up about seeing Jesus, the other disciples began to see Him, too. He appeared inside that locked room and brought peace in the midst of their terror.

Your journey down the path of life has not been a mistake. The Lord knew the road you would take. He knows the things overwhelming you. He knows you can't make sense of it all. He's already been walking with you and now wants you to see Him clearly. Soon, you will know how to help others see Jesus!

This book will not present mere factoids (tedious information) about a historical figure. You are entering the operating room for corrective vision surgery. Don't worry! Jesus is the Great Physician and He can remove the cataracts or stigmatisms that have kept you from seeing as you should.

If you and I had seen Him in the flesh back at that time, we probably would not have noticed Him. One official spokesperson said that Jesus had no "magnificence that we should see Him; nor form that we should desire Him."[3] He just wasn't one to catch your eye, I guess. I fear I would have rejected Him the way too many did.

As we move forward, you will discover that you can "see" Him better than anyone did while He walked on earth. I know that sounds impossible right now, but as we gaze at Him, you will find it much more than a museum experience. As you glimpse Him, you will find Him looking back at you. Through our journey you will develop a closer connection with Him, hearing from Him, and He hearing you.

If you ever wished to live in Jesus's time and to have known Him personally, this is your opportunity. As this book begins to immerse us in the Gospels, we will experience the deep

---

[3] Isaiah 53:2, LITV.

bond His original followers built with Him.4 Traumas and wounds leave us empty and confused, but Jesus brings peace and a sense of expectancy in life.

Want a joyful, fulfilling life? One of His key eyewitnesses promised, "We write these things to you that your joy may be full."5 We will examine those eyewitness reports and discover His biography changing our daily lives.

You don't have to be a physical eyewitness to see Jesus. One writer who did not physically see Jesus said that "we do see Jesus crowned with glory and honor."6 We will be seeing beyond what eyes glimpse, as we continue "looking to the Author and Finisher of our faith, Jesus."7

In an attempt to have a clear view of the Scriptures, I will be quoting a lot from a remake of the *King James Version* entitled the *Literal Translation of the Holy Bible.*8 This version gets us closer to the original sense of the text with more modern language. The wording of the biblical quotes in this book may sound unfamiliar to you because we are using the *Lit Translation*, as I like to call it.

I recommend that you read one chapter of this book each day. It will take you about a month at that pace. You can binge-read it in one day if you like. However, the message will soak in better and last for the long term if taken in small doses.

To enhance your journey through the gospels, get the accompanying *Seeing Jesus Handbook* (download or printed

---

4 In I John 1:3, one of His eyewitnesses said that these events were recorded so we could have partnership and participation with them and thus with Him.

5 I John 1:4, LITV.

6 Hebrews 2:9, LITV. Even before Jesus came, people walked in faith as "seeing the Invisible One" (Hebrews 11:27, LITV).

7 Hebrews 12:2, LITV.

8 This is the translation by Jay Green, Sr., not *Young's Literal Translation* of 1898.

version). Be sure you have your favorite Bible handy. The handbook will help you process every verse in the Gospels at your own pace as we move forward.

As you journal your progress in seeing Jesus and understanding His plans for you, that handbook will become a "Gospel According to You." It will be your accounts of walking with the Master. You will probably come to treasure that volume more than this one because it will document your development.

My prayer for you during our time together on these pages is that the Lord will "give to you a spirit of wisdom and revelation in the full knowledge of Him." 9 I pray you become a new person, with "the eyes of your mind having been enlightened."10 Now, with open eyes and open hearts, we begin *Seeing Jesus*!

---

9 Ephesians 1:17, LITV.
10 Ephesians 1:18, LITV.

KEEP SECRETS MUCH?

Foreword

HAVE YOU EVER HAD SOMEONE blab a secret that you didn't want anyone else knowing? Have you had a surprise ruined because someone forgot and told the wrong person about it? Sometimes, I have been guilty of that.

Leaking secrets is big business these days. Corporations leak secrets as a marketing strategy or to test the market. For example, a leaked secret tested the public to see if we would be excited about buying a $1,000 phone (I'm still laughing). Other times a business teases by releasing part of the information or leaking it out in a way the competition misunderstands. The dog-food-giant Ralston allegedly faked out their competitors with a hint that sent them investing their funds in the wrong direction.[11]

The narrative of the Bible shows the Creator's info-leaks marketing strategy. Communications from Headquarters randomly slipped out details about the big changes coming. Throughout the Scriptures, there are dropped hints and outright

---

[11] Ian McGrath, et al, "We're Leaking, and Everything's Fine: how and why companies deliberately leak secrets," Academia.edu, 1998.

spoilers about the coming Hero. Pasting those together, we could surmise that a certain ruler and rescuer would change everything about the world.

The competition chased after the wrong thing. Had the Lord's enemies understood the mystery, they would have played a different role.[12] Instead, the dark forces played into His strategy!

The Old Testament is a series of leaks of classified info. As some of the oldest writings in human possession, the Scriptures tell us a man like Jesus was coming and to watch for Him. The heavenly Publisher commissioned His writers and poets those thousands of years ago to tell about Him. Without fail, every white paper, biography, song, or ballad He produced hinted something on the topic of Jesus.

Though there were no Wikileaks at that time, God dripped clues through His anchors. For example, Isaiah spilled part of the message to the people: "For unto us a Child is born, unto us a Son is given." Not only would a child come, but He would rule and be called, "Wonderful Counselor, Mighty God, Everlasting Father, Prince of Peace."[13] Many do not understand this part of the secret.

When we come to Matthew, Mark, Luke, and John, we have the official press releases. The New Testament reads like a disclosure manual on the greatest improvement in human history. It also includes leaked info on the next big "launch."

We want to get the story from the source and not only hear what spiritual pundits say about the press releases. Too many Bible thumpers take random tweets or 30-second clips from corporate and tell us what to think about them. We want the whole thing. We want to know the topic and context of that public service announcement. Until we understand what these

---

[12] See I Corinthians 2:6-7. We will talk about this concept in future books.
[13] Isaiah 9:6, a paraphrase.

things meant to the original hearers, we cannot fully connect how they apply to us.

"Christian" kookism and crazy misunderstandings run wild. Many Christians feel satisfied to "heart" God's status updates and "like" His memes. They remind me of people who don't want to see the whole movie but will quote the cool lines as if they've been there.

You and I want the whole scoop, not just a "taste" here and there. People who call themselves "believers" should at least want to sit down at the restaurant. Too many are living on aromas instead of filling up on the bread of Life and the meat of the Word. We, however, are hungry.

One should comb the Bible like an investigator would a sensitive data release by Julian Assange, catching clues and discovering top-secret revelations. However, raw info always comes from some context that will help us understand it better. From the beginning, humans often miss the truth. Here are some examples of leaked sound bites:

"A snake smasher is coming."[14]

The first woman looked for a promised offspring who would stomp the serpent (the source of sin and evil on earth). If she thought this hero was her firstborn son, she was sadly disappointed. Afterward, women everywhere hoped one of their sons would be the promised one to solve it all.

"The Anointed Prince will come with power."[15]

Passages that spoke of a Messiah indicated a great ruler would come. The people began looking for a King or powerful military leader.

---

[14] See Genesis 3:15. These are not exact quotes, just tweet-size summaries.
[15] See Daniel 9:25.

"A suffering servant will take abuse."[16]

This leak left many thinking about the condition of their nation instead of a person like Jesus. They could not understand how a hero would be both a servant and a king.

God planned out this plot before the dawn of time. It should shock us: make us laugh, make us cry. If the Gospel message does not move you, then you missed something. If you only see a Caucasian Jesus with hair blowing in the wind, you have been lied to. If your Jesus is a weapon for Bible battles, you have been baited and hooked. Is He caged in by polarized religious groups each guarding their own "recipe"?

We could spend weeks looking at the various religious filters in our world and how they distorted bits of leaked info. We will be healthier, though, and find it more exciting to look at the official interpreters of that leaked info. The Gospels (the first four books of the New Testament) give not only the history of Jesus but serve as the official commentary on those leaks. These individuals lived as eyewitnesses to the fulfillment of all those posts, spoilers, and tweets from the previous 4,000 years.

Typically, a person views one Gospel at a time—or in little pieces like a random newsfeed of tweets and snaps (snapshots, pics, whatever). Through this tour, we will bring those four journalists together as a collage to show us everything in the order of how it all happened. With this quartet of historians, we will discover truths that can reshape our daily lives, no matter how long any of us has been religious, or not.

Now, watch the process of how gently the Lord introduces His master plan to humanity. In the coming pages, you will see that He has been working in your life, too, even when you did not

---

[16] See Isaiah 42:1; 52:13; 53:1-11.

notice. So, let's begin our adventure to get the whole message, not just pieces.

EPIC PICS

YOU AND I HAVE JUST LANDED in Israel. The heat outside seems to come from above and beneath all at the same time. Headquarters, silent for over 400 years, will soon release something worth significant coverage: the promised One is almost here.

We notice some guys getting off our plane whom we discover to be video and photojournalists. They are carrying all kinds of gear, and although they know about each other, all four are working independently, for the most part. Their assignment is to help us see Jesus.

The young man assembling his boom mic with that wind-proof "dead cat" cover[17] is called Mark. He has a knack for capturing dramatic moments and getting his camera right into the middle of the action. As we review his footage, you will love the breathtaking glimpses he gives us of Jesus. Even though he does not have a big team, Mark's director, Rocky, will give him the close-up access he needs for us to see the best cinematic effects.

---

[17] A "dead cat" is a furry sleeve put over a microphone so the wind does not make distracting noises in a recording.

Our next and most epic producer is Matt. He's not making a movie for the general public but intends to help his fellow Jews to see. Thus it's rated "J" not "G." It isn't exclusive though. He doesn't mind if we sit in on his production, but he works specifically to meet his audience's viewing compatibilities. Of course, he knows that many of them will be upset when they examine Jesus through his lens. Good journalists get the facts and present an honest reality, regardless of what the public will say. Those who find his work offensive will have a clear picture of what upset them.

Next, is a sharply dressed man who does not appear to know his way around Israel as well as the others. He wasn't born here and some say he is not even Jewish. Luke's documentary will provide very detailed reporting on the Messiah. He has the biggest team working with him and will interview many more people than can make the screen. Luke does not capture only high-drama moments but also goes backstage often. He shows us the outsiders. He cameos several women in his work and gives them a fair balance of screen time. But this is no chick-flick. Luke also does not intend for this to be a one-off production; his blockbuster feeds into the sequel which we will have to sit down and view together sometime as well.[18]

Last, John does not carry much equipment. He works alone. Sometimes he does his own stunts, though you will not see his name in the credits. He's a modest fellow. The striking difference between John and the others is that he is not carrying a video recorder. He clips his 45 megapixel DSLR camera onto a stand and snaps on a massive zoom lens. He spends hours setting up to capture the right scene. The timing has to be just right: location, lighting, angle, and subjects. Of course, the autofocus is set on the Man from Nazareth, but the other

---

[18] The author of the Gospel of Luke is also the author of the Book of Acts, which builds on the themes begun in that Gospel narrative. Watch for my coming series that will begin with Acts.

characters we find in John's frames will help us see Jesus in a distinct way from what the other journalists do.

Might you think one of these guys is not necessary? I mean, after all, aren't they going to repeat each other's work? Won't they be bumping into each other and crowding the shots? Well, there are a couple of times where one producer comes into view on another's screen, but that helps to keep it real. By compiling their works into one saga, we find more than just a one-dimensional version of Jesus. This is more real than "reality television" (an oxymoron for sure). Better than 3D, this film festival will beat any virtual reality adventure with a little help from the Star of the show Himself.

Which picture will we start with? Well, Mark would be fun. He begins right in the middle of the action, focused on a rough-looking outdoorsman yelling into the camera.[19] We could start with this fine introduction to Jesus. Luke, however, goes back further and spotlights the parents of that man from the wilderness. A lot of people yawn their way through this episode because they think it is just B-roll filling time to get us past the opening credits. However, those introductory scenes set the stage for all that happens in the main show. We'll get to that soon, so don't walk in late.

Matthew's opening sequence reaches back even further, with slides of Jewish legends including Father Abraham and King David.[20] Right away, his Hebrew followers know this is no ordinary flick because we get a longer glimpse of some godless members of that supporting cast—Tamar, her sex life had blacklisted her; Ruth, she came from a godless place; Rahab, a former prostitute; and, though not named directly, Bathsheba, who had a child with King David while married to one of his warriors.[21] Yes, if you were not on the edge of your seat already,

---

[19] See Mark 1:1-4.
[20] See Matthew 1:1-17.
[21] Was Bathsheba raped? Was she an adulteress? We won't get sidetracked with that discussion right now, but the fact that we are asking those

17

you probably have spilled some popcorn. If these kinds of people are in the intro, what will this main narrative be about?

To summarize these intros:

- Mark begins with Jesus's ministry.
- Matthew takes us back to the beginning of everything Hebrew.
- Luke reaches even farther, in a later clip, to the beginning of humanity, Adam.[22]
- John—master of the still shot—takes us to the best opening scene of all time: "In the beginning."[23]

Let's view Jesus in the order everything happened. Deal? We will let all four voices inform us together.

People often see Jesus through filters such as religions, denominations, personal experiences, or pop theologians. The Jesus most people see looks as pixilated as the lousy image in an annoying chain message that should have died in 2005. After mass efforts at sharing, sharing, sharing Him, Christianity has reduplicated Christ into a sketchy copy with little clarity. We need to see again through the clear view of these authorized producers.

It is one thing to read a map and another to know the location. While driving across the country once, my wife and I decided we wanted some pizza. Our online search showed us a place with rave reviews that led us on a drive to downtown Toledo after dark. Parking on the street, I glanced at the

---

questions shows what a shocker it is for her to be listed in the genealogy of this Man we want to focus on. Her name and others were included to make us squirm, to shatter the idea that life is always clinical and orthodox, and to show us that God can make good things come even from a messy past.

[22] See Luke 3:23-38.

[23] John 1:1 and Genesis 1:1.

buildings noticing the lights of a bar or two. I was not very comfortable leaving my family sitting there at the curb for long, but I ran inside to get the goods. A drunk staggered past my family in our Suburban a few times. I began to wonder if this was a good idea.

After a wait, I took our two boxes of deep-dish Chicago-style pizza in hand. It was a sacred moment—almost spiritual. The uncomfortable feeling with being in this area gave way to joyous rapture with the first bite. We had never had such inch-deep flavors of sauce, meat, and cheese. And the buttery, flakey crust! How unexpected and totally awesome—like a marriage between Italy and a croissant. Instantly, I added this to my list of what Heaven must be like.

Okay, I am exaggerating a little—except for the part about the holy shiver I felt when I took those boxes in hand. That happened.

I tell you this story in all its flavor to make this point: anyone can find Pizzapapalis on Google Maps. You could zoom to street-view and "walk" among the same buildings. You could look at dozens of pictures of those better-than-Chicago pizzas.[24] But none of that would be the same as actually tasting one.

I want to see Jesus, not Yelp reviews or 3D street views. I don't want a Jesus assembled from soundbites and insta-stories. I want to connect with the true Person, not pictures. No filters. No layer masks. No pixelation. We just want to see Jesus.

I once thought my lens of Jesus was adequate enough. I thought I knew the Gospels. I had grown up with Christian schooling. My parents' traveling ministry took me to over 200

---

[24] My friends in the Detroit area will confirm if you doubt my assessment here. Pizzapapalis does Chicago-style better than Chicago. And yes, I've eaten pizza at the big-name place in Chicago. Thank you for reading this promo. It was unsolicited. I am just doing my part to make the world aware of the genius of using a flakey pastry crust on pizza. You're welcome.

churches, seminars, and conferences by the time I turned 15. I read theological books for fun. Yet the Lord called me to reboot in my young adult years.

Crisis, you could call it. I hit a wall and I could not define it. No, I did not get into drugs, gangs, or prison, but I hit a struggle we all face.

I wanted my life to mean something.

A series of events jerked me awake from the stupor of a monotonous life. At this point, I was a few years into a great marriage with my beautiful wife Leanne. We had a few lovable children, a successful business venture, and great health. Still, I crashed. Life had become too predictable.

Was I here to pay bills, eat meals, and breathe oxygen? There had to be more to life. I had to do something worthwhile, not just exist.

Leanne and I began to talk to Jesus more. We began taking shifts of watching the children while the other prayed. We were being drawn by the Lord and did not know exactly to what or why, but we were ready for this chase.

We were happily involved in our local church. I knew a lot about God. I could defend Him with my memorized Bible verses and try to convince others of how they should believe. Church activities were central to everything I did.

When this longing began—I was not sure what to call it— the Lord was calling me to Himself, but in my head I was searching to find me. I thought I knew Him. I had all that Bible stuff figured out. I'm not joking. I used to watch religious debates as a teenager and the only books I ever bought were Bible reference works.

I have discovered that I am not alone in my pursuit to know my true identity. That longing stirs deeply inside us all. Unfortunately, it is often suppressed. Society tells us what to be, how to think, what to laugh at, and how to be accepted. Much "Christian culture" also becomes groupthink to the expense of individuality. We all tend to feed into the center of some system where conformity is necessary for survival.

I didn't want to be a clone. My driving question was, "God, what is your plan for my life?" It might have been a little self-focused, but at least I was heading in the right direction for an answer.

The inner gnawing continued. Days of fasting. Prayer. Reading the Scriptures. Reading missionary books. Talking to people of deep prayer. Asking spiritual heroes to help me sort this out, to help me find me. That sounds sick now when I say it that way, but there was more to this than finding me (which by itself would have been a very short trip).

I moved out of my comfort zone. I could not really explain it to anyone but there was something more I had to have. Something I had to do.

I. Had. To. Know. Jesus.

That's what was driving me. My quest to find my life purpose was really a desire to know Him. I just had not realized it at the time.

Are you there now? I hope so.

I went to a mobile home out in the middle of nowhere. Okay, in Oklahoma. But it was as close to nowhere as I could travel at the time. My wife and children went and stayed with her family for a few weeks.

There I sat alone to pray, think, read, and seek. It wasn't a cabin by a mountain stream, but there I could sit and listen to the whirl of grasshopper wings in the hot air. I could pray while inhaling the aroma of chicken houses and cow pastures. I could pore through the Scriptures and pause to watch the occasional

21

pickup truck stir up a cloud of silty, red dust on that lonely country lane.

I laugh thinking about how extreme it was to be sitting out in the middle of nowhere for weeks without a vehicle. I know the Lord led me to that. There was no external crisis looming. Our health was all good.

I had to get away from the distractions, from the noise, and just reboot. My wife was drawn, too, but she did not have to go through as much to get to where she needed to be in the Lord. I've always been harder headed than she is. So, she gave me the space to plow through.

I knew what deep prayer was. The Lord had guided me in other areas of life before, but this was different. The spiritual craving would not stop. My soul was like a dog staring at sizzling burgers on the backyard grill.

Humbling myself there, I entered a new realm of prayer. Every breath, every moment of the day, I was able to step instantly in the presence of God. Talking to Him became as easy as breathing.

Then, one day, it happened.

I saw Jesus.

I had come here looking to understand my life, my purpose, my calling, to see me. But I saw Him.

I am not going to tell you that Jesus appeared to me in the flesh. Such visions do happen occasionally, but that is not what this book is about. This is not a manual for how to conjure up a visit from the Man from Galilee.

Sorry. Not sorry.

In that moment I realized He did not need me defending Him with my razor-sharp Bible skills. He can hold His own. I realized that the One I had memorized so many verses about was real, personal, and present.

I have tried explaining that experience to a few people—what I felt, what happened inside me, but words don't do the job. I have finally realized it is not about sharing what I experienced but about helping others see Jesus for themselves. That's why we are here together right now.

Are you trying to figure your life out? Are you trying to understand who you are? Those, among others, are God-given questions that lead you to Him. Once we view Him, the other questions are not a struggle.

Don't worry; I did not come back with some crazy religion or a bizarre practice I'm going to try to get you to follow. In fact, getting close to the Lord was somehow simplifying. Even a child can follow Him.

Your story will be different than mine. Your experiences are your own. The new insights and understanding you gain on this journey will be yours to enjoy and share with Him and others who know Him. You will see Him for yourself and find answers to your questions and inner longings.

What happened for me on the backside of nowhere could have happened a whole lot easier if my eyes had been open. In fact, what we can discover in the Gospels has done more for me than that isolated spiritual experience ever could. All that drama of moving out of my home, leaving my job, and temporarily escaping society only helped me remove my blindfolds. I could see Jesus easily after that.

In the lives of common men, women, and children, Jesus shows up. They not only see Jesus for themselves but they let others see Him through them. We are a growing army.

Life is about seeing Jesus, yet the busyness and distractions tend to hide Him. The harder we try, the more we seem to complicate it. You don't have to take a sabbatical in

Oklahoma. You can't stay at my "shrine" anyway because that trailer home is gone now. Instead, I want to invite you into a portal to another word: the Kingdom.

Though my "take off the blindfold" moment happened many years ago, I am still seeing Jesus better as I continue into His realm. When I had that eye-opening moment, I thought that would be all I needed. I didn't realize how much there was to see of Him. One great experience with the Lord does not magically change a person forever. I went through some low times after that. I've also had many, many more awakening moments where I saw deeper into the realm of the King.

Seeing Jesus changed me at the very core. I had deeply-rooted flaws. Selfishness, pride, and a whole bunch of other evils mangled my spirit, but I put on a suit and looked good at Christian gatherings. The real problems weren't so much that I had areas to improve, as everyone has, but that I was blind to my own defects. My wife would plead with me to not be so severe and friends would try to steady me in areas I was off-base, but I just couldn't see it.

Even that explosive experience alone in prayer and fasting didn't change all that. What has changed me is the continual pursuit of seeing Jesus. The more I see Him in Scripture, in prayer, and in the little things of daily life, the more light He has shone on my life and I see where I have been unlike Him. Better, He has given me the power to overcome flaws I did not even realize I had back then!

My marriage has changed, my parenting changed, my love for people grew, and so many other areas improved, too. No self-help book has helped me like getting a clear view of Jesus has. I know the same will happen for you, too, in whatever area you need to improve. I cannot give the answer to every issue, but I can point you to Him.

I imagine you have brushed up against God from time to time. Maybe you were looking for Him; maybe you just got in His way. This time, let's catch the whole view of Him, how He sees things, and how we should.

I wish I could say I have discovered it all now and am here to tell you every detail you need to know. Instead, I want to invite you on the journey. I don't want to tell you about the destination but walk with you as we get there. We are going to start over from the beginning and reexamine everything from the start.

This is not a mystical voyage to find new information or an emotional jag to trigger chill bumps on your arms. We will follow the Way that Jesus authorized for us to know Him, the Gospels. This premier will remove your blindfolds. Brace yourself, the light could be stronger than you expected at first.

There is much more to Jesus than your physical eyes could show you. If you are willing to let things go that will block your view of Him, then we can do this. If you want Him more than anything, then we are on the same path.

Are you ready?

I am confident you are because you have come this far. Turn to the next page as we give the Gospel a fresh start in our lives!

WHEN TIME IS AGAINST YOU

IF YOU ARE AT THE RETIREMENT center, you don't mention to your shuffleboard friends that you are hoping to have a child someday. At the Scrabble and Seniors' picnic, you don't ask your friends to pray that you could one day have a boy. If you are living on your retirement investments and Social Security, you aren't decorating a bedroom in either blue or pink. If you've not had kids by that point, you most likely have given up on the idea.

That's where Liz and Zack were.[25] It had been so long since they wanted a child that they forgot they did. Time had moved on, leaving her arms empty and his face unlit with the pride of having a boy.[26] To their friends, they were just Elizabeth and Zachariah—that couple in Hebron who never had any kids.

Only Luke gives us footage of the interactions in this unlikely home. At first glance, they don't feel like they belong under the lights, but God staged this event for a reason. Looking at this narrative gives us insights into how the Lord works in us today.

---

[25] They probably were not members of a retirement center. See their story for yourself at Luke 1:5.

[26] See Luke 1:7.

But why? Why would the Lord not give them a child? Well, the word on the street—and in the "churches" of their day—said it was because they had done something wrong. The religious talking-heads theorized a series of cause and effect scenarios. Looking at what problem you had, they would assume it indicated what sin you had committed.

You can be sure it was embarrassing for Liz and Zack to walk by the city park where all their parenting friends were hanging out and talking. It hurt to watch their friends' kids play in the loose sand or climb the swaying trees. Perhaps they struggled with a little envy when they looked at happy families.

To the moral theorists of the time, not having children was a sign someone had been sexually devious. Gossips talked behind Elizabeth's back about what she must have done that her parents never found out about. However, Liz was a virgin when she married. She had to be or she could not have married a priest.[27]

What had these two done that was so bad? Nothing. They had not done anything against the covenant of Moses. They had lived good lives and everyone respected their discipline. Even God called them blameless![28]

Still, they had this problem—they could not have a child. Living right does not make life perfect and painless. We cannot assume that because someone is having a hard time they are doing evil. Sometimes godly people go through some junk and do not know why until later, if ever. We cannot see the details behind the scenes. This couple must have struggled emotionally knowing the Scriptures promised God would bless those who lived right. They lived by the commands but had not seen the promises.

---

[27] See Leviticus 21:14.
[28] See Luke 1:6.

This matters to you and me because there are blind spots in our lives that are out of our control. Some things the Lord does not want us to see yet. This wonderful husband and wife had done nothing to deserve walking through life with this black hole in their experience. If you find yourself in a confusing time, don't beat yourself up for the things you don't understand. I wrote that for myself, but you are welcome to take it personally, too.

Although this Mr. and Mrs. had forgotten their desire for a child, Someone else had not. In fact, there was a reminder of the Never-Forgetter in Zachariah's name. It means "Yahweh remembers." And He did, even though old Zack had forgotten.

Our story picks up at the Temple. Since it shows up in many scenes, let's take a quick tour of the panorama. In the northwest corner of Jerusalem, this massive building rose 60 feet in the air. Made of white marble, the ground level had roofed walkways forming a rectangle around it.

An aroma of barbequed meat rose from the courtyard in front of the building entrance as Temple workers offered sacrifices. Only staff and officials could set foot on this hallowed ground. At the perimeter of the altar area, Jewish men gathered to watch and to worship. Another walled section formed an open-air square called the Court of the Women where Jewish women (and men) could enter. Beyond that, the Court of the Gentiles spread into a gigantic area where anyone could come within the parameters of the covered walkways all around.

To look inside the Temple, if you were allowed, would have amazed you. Its giant doors and thick curtains made quite a statement. The golden furniture beat any home makeover ever.

Entering there was Zack's once-in-a-lifetime opportunity. His tribal heritage privileged him to stand before the golden altar inside and offer incense, which lifted as a sweet aroma to the Lord.[29] The people waited and worshipped outside while he did

---

[29] See Luke 1:8-9.

this.³⁰ When he finished, he would go out and pronounce a blessing over them all.

Boom! An angel showed up and said, "Do not be afraid."³¹

Zack did not obey.

It is a funny thing when Heaven touches earth. God comes down to cheer us up, but we thank Him by having a panic attack. The elderly priest focused on breathing and keeping his heart pumping while the angel told him he had words of joy.³²

Today, people often experience something similar when they sense God's presence for the first time. One man said he wanted to run. Another said he wanted to hide. But the Lord reveals Himself in power like this because He wants to bring us joy. And, because He wants us to know He hears us.

The angel tells Zack, "Your prayer was heard."

I imagine this guy is thinking to himself, "What prayer? I haven't been asking for anything."

The angel explained further, "Your wife Elizabeth will bear you a son."

Bam! Zack was scared before; now he's in shock. He's thinking, "A baby? Now?" I can hear him mutter under his breath, "It's a little late, isn't it? I mean, why couldn't you have—"

"You will call his name Yochanan—'favored of Yahweh.'" In our language, the name is simply John.

At this moment, Zack's mind must have done a little calculating. What are the odds that he would be here this day? Some priests never got picked to offer incense in the Temple in

---

³⁰ See Luke 1:10.
³¹ See Luke 1:11-13.
³² See Luke 1:14.

their lifetime. Of the 18,000 priests alive then,[33] what was the chance that he would be picked? Could this message have been for someone else? Was the timing random or precise?

This was the epic moment of Zack's life. Burning incense on that altar may have been a once-in-a-lifetime experience because priests only got to do this once and only if the "dice" fell their way. This does not look so random after all. The Lord not only chose him to offer worship, but He sent a messenger to him. Zack blinked and looked again to convince himself that there really was an angel standing there in front of him, between the golden altar and the lampstand. There was.

"But when did I last pray for a child?" he thought. He had let go of those dreams long ago. But, he had just prayed. That is what a priest did for all those dear people outside, those wonderful people who also loved the Lord and were so oppressed.

The theme of Zack's prayer came back to him. He had been praying for their deliverance. "Oh Lord," he likely had cried, "take us out of the grasp of our enemies. Come save your people! Rescue us, great God of Abraham." That prayer? How did having a boy named John answer that prayer?

The angel boomed, "And he will be joy and gladness to you, and many will rejoice over his birth."[34] This one would help bring the salvation that Zachariah had petitioned the Lord for. God heard his prayer and answered on His own schedule. God does not live by our agenda. Just because something He promised hasn't happened does not mean it won't. His timing is different than our timing.

When your answer finally shows up, will you remember what you asked for? Maybe your hopes have started to slip. Has

---

[33] Leon Morris, *Luke: An Introduction and Commentary*, Tyndale New Testament Commentaries, Vol. 3, (Downers Grove, IL: 1988).
[34] Luke 1:14, LITV.

weariness caused your dreams to fade? Or will you keep believing? Follow along with this elderly man (and others) to see how his promise, like yours, will unfold.

FACTS AGAINST TRUTH

E XPERTS ONCE LAUGHED at the idea of anyone making a machine that could fly. Speaking of the impossible, Dr. Moses Judah Folkman (1933-2008) pioneered biological discoveries in an arena where other experts told him nothing could be done. In the early 1970s, the idea of angiogenesis (new blood vessels growing in the human body) baffled the medical minds of his time, but Folkman pressed on. He believed and eventually proved that tumors develop their own arteries to stay alive. When proven later, his research provided the foundation for therapies that would either inhibit blood vessel growth in cancer patients or stimulate it in heart patients.[35]

Dr. Folkman kept a copy of a 1903 article where two physics professors gave "proof" why it would be impossible to create a flying aircraft. The New York Times published that article three months before the world-changing flight at Kitty Hawk, North Carolina.[36] Encouraged by the flight of the impossible, Folkman changed the way modern doctors think about the growth of arteries.

God works in the realm of the impossible. Most people never see what He is doing behind the scenes because they are

---

[35] "Judah Folkman," Wikipedia.org/wiki/Judah_Folkman
[36] Fran Lostys, "You're Studying Dirt," The Reader's Digest, July 2005.

only tuned into the realm of "here and now." Zack was not an innovator. He was not here to change the system—he was just glad to be a part of it. To him, the angel's announcement sounded as wild as angiogenesis or flying ox carts.

Not only did the angel announce that the elderly couple would have a son, but that this son would be a world-changer. The Lord would see him as great,[37] he would never touch a drop of alcohol,[38] the Spirit would fill him before his birth,[39] he would turn people toward the Lord,[40] and he would go in the power of Elijah to prepare people for the Lord's arrival.[41] He would restore relationships by turning the hearts of fathers back toward their children and the hearts of fools to listen to the right-living ones! Zack would hold a baby who would steer many to see the Lord!

At this point, you want Zack to jump for joy and claim his miracle. He could have shouted, "Won't He do it!"

But our man responds, "Wait... what? I can't even."

The impossibilities are mounting in his mind. "Us? How did we qualify for something like this? Maybe this message is for someone else. Perhaps God doesn't realize our situation." He blurts out, "How is that supposed to happen? Look, I'm an old man. My wife—she's gotten up in years, too."

---

[37] See Luke 1:15 which connects to the Malachi 3:1 phrase "before the Lord." One part of this prophecy comes to fulfillment in Matthew 11:11 and Luke 7:28 when Jesus calls John the greatest prophet up to that time.
[38] See Numbers 6:4-5. While there is connection here to the requirements of the Nazarite vow, John was not to keep his hair uncut as Sampson. Those who portray John as having long hair have misrepresented the man and potentially effeminized a rugged country bloke.
[39] John had a special allotment of the Spirit and in a different way than was possible before Pentecost. The Spirit would come upon prophets often to prophesy and do the work. To prepare the core group of disciples Jesus would train, John had to be led of the Spirit.
[40] See Luke 1:16.
[41] See Luke 1:17 with Isaiah 40:3 and Malachi 4:5-6.

When was the last time you had one of those "So, look, God, that's not possible" conversations? Telling the Inventor of everything that something is impossible seems quite ridiculous. That kind of faith will never see the promise fulfilled.

We base our sense of impossible on our perceptions. We observe, measure, weigh, explore, and then form conclusions from our limited abilities. What we call "laws" of nature are established patterns we have measured and observed with our senses. What if there are other methods of investigation? What if God sees everything differently than we do? For us to tell Him how things are is like the vision-impaired man describing the sunset or the hearing-impaired man teaching someone to sing.

The angel explained what will happen. The human did not realize how special it was for God to include him in what He was doing. Somehow he thinks he will improve the situation by pointing out the inconsistencies. The heavenly being has to explain to the human being that he did not make up the plan: "I am Gabriel, who stands before God, and I was sent to speak to you and to announce to you the good news of these things."[42]

This is not looking good for Zack.

Wham! The angel then struck the man with silence. Zack's mouth had killed the moment of his miracle. Apparently when God does His work, He does not want His people talking it down. Not only does the Lord work in the realm where everything is possible, but He also works in the realm of faith—accepting as "done" things that have not yet happened. Zack was not in tune with either of those.

Notice the angel's reason for hitting "mute" on Zacharias's mouth: "You did not believe my words which shall be fulfilled in their own season."[43] A believer needs to accept God's timing and His out-of-the-ordinary ways of doing things. Of course, things

[42] Luke 1:19, LITV.
[43] Luke 1:20, LITV.

will surprise us, but when shock turns to resistance, we have stepped into a danger zone.

Zack wasn't alone in his disbelief. Other people have questioned their miracle. Hebrew heroes like Gideon and Hezekiah each asked for a sign. The legendary couple Abraham and Sarah laughed when they heard their good news of a late-in-life child. Why were they not struck mute? Because Zack is emphatic with his self-identity as being unable to do this.[44]

Zack as much as says, "I am impotent," to the representative of the omnipotent One. The angel came to declare good news. He had to silence Zack from his bad news.

This priest comes stumbling out to the people who had begun to wonder what was taking him so long. Instead of being able to bless them, he can say nothing. What about us? Do I wring my hands in worry? If I cannot claim the identity God has for me, how can I access the blessings?

The good things from above come when we believe God's promises. Like Zack, when I do not believe what God plans for me, I rob others of how I was to benefit them, too. Think if he could have come out and told the story of what God was going to do. Imagine the faith it would have stirred among these faithful worshippers!

God's definition of reality differs from ours. He has no health limitations. He has no financial limitations. We must not limit Him to what we know.

Life and death are in the power of the tongue.[45] That's why Zack's lips were sealed. I, too, have endangered my own destiny by talking out of turn. What have you "talked smack" about? Have you criticized plans God has for you? What about your joy? Have you claimed sorrow, depression, hopelessness? What about

---

[44] Morris, *Luke*, TNTC 3.
[45] See Proverbs 18:21.

love? Have you claimed, "I cannot help but dislike that person?" What about faith? Have you said you cannot see how He would provide?

Take a moment and reflect on your situation. Where have you rejected things God wanted to bring to life for you? What impossibilities do you need to go back and pick up at the altar?

UNEXPECTED SPOTLIGHT

T O HELP US SEE THE RIGHT RESPONSE to God's plan, Luke zooms in on two women. In that time, women were the supporting cast in society; very few stepped into the spotlight. Luke, the inspired fact-recorder, shows us women who played key roles at the beginning of the Gospel. The Creator gave a foundational role to the woman at the beginning of history, too.[46]

This new reality did not simply "allow" women a place; they start and finish the narrative of Jesus's life. Beyond just birthing children, the women's words of faith speak to us today louder than Zachariah's unbelief. Watch this scene unfold.

Enter Elizabeth. She has endured hurtful gossip all her life because she was not able to have a child.[47] Both the Bible and history show us that her community would have objectified her for being barren, childless. When she realized she was pregnant, she kept it a secret for five months! Can you imagine the looks on the faces of her quilting friends when she finally came out in public?

---

[46] See Genesis 1:28. God gave dominion authority to the man and the woman together.
[47] See Luke 1:23-24.

She saw her pregnancy as a gift from God, not as a hassle. Too often, people complain about children as if they were a hindrance rather than a joy, as the Creator intended them to be for us. Our offspring are God's compensation to us and a powerful force for defeating the enemy.[48]

Publicly shamed for not having children, Liz's embarrassment began to lift when the Lord sent her this John-boy. She praised Him for noticing her. She recognized that He was taking away her reproach and disgrace.[49]

Next, we meet a young woman as Gabriel appears to her in Nazareth. Before we learn the name of this key female, the opening scene introduces her to us first with the word "virgin."[50] Mary's character precedes her name. The Lord has noticed her commitment and the angel says so, "Rejoice, highly favored one, the Lord is with you; blessed are you among women!"[51]

We already know Gabriel from his visit to Zachariah in the Temple. But that wasn't his first cameo. Old Gabe had appeared to a prophet named Daniel many, many years before and announced the coming of the Messiah.[52] Here this angel arrives again, announcing the same Man.

Mary does not react much differently than old Zack. At Gabe's command to rejoice, she panics. The appearance of an angel took her by surprise, as much as it would any of us.[53] As typical after any startling angelic appearance, the angel tells this human to calm down. He reassures the young woman that she has favor from God, not His anger.[54]

---

[48] See Psalm 127:3-5.
[49] See Luke 1:25.
[50] See Luke 1:26-27.
[51] Luke 1:28, from the *New King James Version,* (Thomas Nelson, 1983), used with permission. Hereafter referred to as "NKJV."
[52] See Daniel 9:21, 25.
[53] See Luke 1:29.
[54] See Luke 1:30.

She will birth the promised One. The Son has not been conceived at the moment of their talk, but He was coming soon![55] Gabriel tells Mary that the Child's name will be "Yahweh-Saves," or in English, "Jesus!" He will rule the people of Israel and a Kingdom with no limits of time or space. She knew that such a King was coming but never realized she would be His mother.

Although I have not always sought favor with God, I rejoice to know that I, too, can become personally connected to this King. You and I are not mere observers. We don't just get to meet this King of everything. Like Mary, we get the shocking realization that we can be close, become family with Him.

Stunned at this impossibility, Mary wonders out loud, "How can this be, seeing I am a virgin?"[56] Zachariah objected that pregnancy was physically impossible for his wife and him. Mary paused at the idea because pregnancy was morally impossible for her, at that point.

The Promised One would arrive this way and only this way. The press release from long ago said that the promised One would come through a virgin.[57] Mary was that person. This is not to say God would have nothing to do with Mary had she lost her virginity, but she could not have been the mother of Jesus.

A believer in her twenties went to see the doctor because of her swollen abdomen. The doctor looked at her and said, "Well, it is obvious that you are pregnant." She responded, "That would have to be a miracle then because I'm a virgin." Tests showed she had an enlarged cyst.

Young women today can have confidence that saving themselves for marriage is still God's plan. For thousands of years, girls of faith kept themselves pure in hopes they could be

---

[55] See Luke 1:31-33 where the Son is described as still to come.
[56] Luke 1:34, WEB.
[57] Isaiah 7:14.

39

the mother of the Messiah. Today also, a believer can keep his or herself pure because of the Messiah.

What about those who deal with shame for sexual sins from the past? The Gospels lead us to heal from that, too. For now, it is good to celebrate Mary—a girl who got it right!

While the Gospel of John gave us some conceptual snapshots to show us Jesus, Luke gives a prenatal image. To Mary, the angel says, "The Holy Spirit will come upon you, and the power of the Most High will overshadow you, and for this reason that Holy One being born of you will be called Son of God."[58] The promise of a late-in-life child astounded humans; this larger-than-life Child astounded angels. This glimpse of Jesus's conception might feel like TMI,[59] but it is need-to-know information. We should not see Jesus as just one of the boys. He is higher and greater from the very start.

Since Mary and Zack both responded to Gabe in a similar way, why wasn't Mary struck silent, too? Zack's question was from a stance of resistance ("I am unable to do this"). Hers was from a place of surprise—as in "How is this possible?" For her, the angel explained how. He did not explain to Zack.

The priest should have believed because he had gray-haired Sarah and wrinkled Abraham as examples. God did the impossible in their lives. Mary had no such precedent, yet she believed.

By the way, Mary, your relative Elizabeth is also living in the miracle level. Why? Because with God nothing is impossible.[60]

The young woman responded differently than the elderly man did: "Let it be just as you have said!"[61] And so it was. Mary

---

[58] Luke 1:35, LITV.
[59] Too much information.
[60] See Luke 1:36-37.
[61] See Luke 1:38.

showed her readiness to embrace the assignment by the life she had lived to this point.

It seems humans usually resist the Lord's desires for our lives at first. Is it that awful to hear from heaven? Is it a bad thing for the Lord to have a plan for your life? "Think of all I'll have to give up" or "I'm not ready for this" are thoughts that want to jump out our lips. Being part of God's plan is so great that a little awkwardness is no big deal.

Many people who reject God's plans for their lives do so because of how afraid they are of what others will think. What if Luke had thought like that and not given us these Scriptures? What if Mary had rejected her calling by being sexually active before marriage? She would have had no part in the events that follow. In order for God to join humanity, a human had to accept His plan for all human lives—sexual purity.

Doing God's will has helped me find my real self in the only way possible (I'm still on that journey). Don't lose what you were designed to be. You will make a difference in the lives of so many others. The life you give the Lord will impact dozens, hundreds, and the ripple effects might reach thousands and millions. Even with something as simple as your sharing this book with someone.[62]

What have you been saying "no" to that you might need to say "yes" to? Answer Him right now, "Let it be to me according to Your Word!"

---

[62] Send a friend to Seeing.Jesusin2020.com to download a free electronic version of *Seeing Jesus*.

SHARE THE WONDER

PERHAPS YOU HAVE BEEN in a school play and had to learn lines from Shakespeare. While you are practicing and preparing, you spend a lot of time with your drama team. You all paint the props in drab colors, put on baggy costumes, and try out curly wigs. You rehearse your lines and practice your roles. You laugh together saying, "Hark" and "Forsooth." Camaraderie develops and you grow to understand each other. If you were to try those same lines with someone on the street, they would think you were odd.

People who live by the promise are few and far between. When you realize your identity with Jesus, you start seeing there are only a few people who understand what you are talking about. This doesn't mean you are better than anyone else—any more than a drama team is better than the rest of a student body. You are simply different in a good way, and you need people in your life who value the same things you value.

You need people on your team who see Jesus. As you go through challenges and struggles, you need to be around others who love Him. Otherwise, you will vent on people who cannot help. Be intentional about who your go-to people will be in your pursuit of Jesus.

The angel told Mary that Elizabeth was also partaking in the mystery. As soon as she heard the angel's words, Mary ran to Elizabeth's house almost 80 miles away.[63] There she would find a woman who would encourage her and understand what she was talking about. Who is your Elizabeth that the Lord has shown you is on the same track?

Who else could Mary talk to? Her mother? Maybe. That would be an awkward conversation. "Mom, I'm pregnant, but it's God's kid, so it's okay." In many ways that conversation was probably not encouraging. Keep in mind that a girl in Mary's day who was sexually active before marriage should have been killed under Moses's law (though death by stoning was not that common by her time).

As your eyes open to Jesus, you will need someone to talk to who understands your journey and will encourage your development. Of course, don't isolate yourself from those who don't know Jesus. Like Mary did with Liz, you will grow stronger by spending time with others who are dedicated to the same pursuit.

When Mary walked into Liz's home, the older woman knew instantly. John, the Spirit-filled baby in her womb, jumped for joy.[64] Then, the power of the Spirit came on Elizabeth and she cried out with a loud voice![65] Getting close to Jesus is not a tame thing.

When you see Jesus, the Spirit becomes activated in your life. God's Spirit moved in Elizabeth powerfully and she spoke out things she could not have known any other way. When you enter the presence of Jesus, His Spirit will confirm it as you speak boldly into the unknown.

---

[63] See Luke 1:39-40.
[64] See Luke 1:41, 44.
[65] See Luke 1:42, LITV.

Liz shouted, "Blessed are you among women!"[66] The word "bless" means to speak uplifting positive things. Cousin Lizzie's words confirmed who Mary was and what she had been chosen to do. When you have Jesus in your life, you need confirmation. You will likely face many who will put you down or do the opposite of blessing: curse you.

When you are chosen, you don't have to announce it. A man I met several years ago went around, saying, "I'm chosen. I'm chosen. I don't know what for, but I'm chosen." When you have a purpose in God's plan (and you do), you don't have to announce it to everyone. The right people will confirm it. Later, you will not be able to hide your purpose. Similar to the way everyone saw Mary's baby bump, the world will see Jesus in you.

Elizabeth also speaks words of life about the Child in Mary's womb. She not only knew Mary was pregnant but also that this Child was the Lord in her! Jews lived in anticipation of the day the Lord would come to His Temple. What that looked like they did not know, but they knew He would come. Now, He has come to Mary's temple.

Becoming a mother changes a woman forever. By being "mother of our Lord," Mary's identity changed and became permanently attached to the Creator. His reputation changed, too. He would now be known as human, submitted to the process He created. When we become connected with Jesus, both our and His roles change—establishing an ongoing family relationship.

Elizabeth celebrated that Mary believed what was "spoken to her from the Lord."[67] She heard from this same Lord whom

_____

[66] Luke 1:42, NKJV.
[67] Luke 1:45, LITV.

44

who now dwelt in her womb.[68] The Lord who speaks to you will also dwell in you.

Liz recognized her in the same way Gabe had, as favored "among women." Never forget that heaven sees your sacrifice. The Lord recognizes the right choices you make when no one else is looking.

After five months in hiding, Elizabeth was ready to face the world. Mary will stay in this safe harbor with her for three months before continuing a whole new life with Jesus in her.[69] Like God called Mary to do great things, so He has a mission for every pure-hearted person today. God blessed her because she believed. He muted Zack because he didn't.

---

[68] See Luke 1:43, 45. Western minds struggle to think of God, the supernatural Being, becoming a human being. The mind of the first-century Middle Easterner thought of supernatural/spirit beings as being able to interact with humans and have human characteristics (Gabriel for example). That being said, the idea of God becoming a baby and growing as an ordinary human was a surprise most of the Bible believers did not see coming.

[69] See Luke 1:56.

REJOICE FOR A REASON

PITCHED HIGH WITH EXCITEMENT, Mary's voice and Lizzie's responded to the wonder of the moment. In that home where a man failed to recognize God's plan and power, the women made up the balance. I imagine warm happy tears trickling down their faces. One with a youthful laugh and the other with crow's-feet wrinkles, as the two women hugged in gladness, one's jet-black curls scrunched against the silver locks of the other.

The young expectant mother took the next turn at praising the Lord. Mary was not conceited that she had received this honor. Calling herself a "slave,"[70] she recognized that she held a lowly place in society and no significance above anyone else.

Mary said, "My soul magnifies the Lord."[71] A magnifying glass helps us see details better and notice things we hadn't seen before. When scrolling through pics on your phone, you spread two fingers to zoom in on some, asking, "What kind of smile was that?" Mary did not hurry this photo-op but paused to zoom her

---

[70] Luke 1:48, LITV.
[71] Luke 1:46, LITV.

focus onto Him.[72] Through this book, we want to magnify the Lord, see Him better, and catch details we have missed.

For Mary, things are different "from now on."[73] Jesus is changing her. She was embracing her new identity because of Him. And because of that, others would see her in a new light. When Jesus enters your life, you have a "from now on" perspective on life.

The more you see Jesus, the more you see yourself differently. If you don't like yourself, see Jesus. Having a hard time seeing Him? Do like Mary and recognize you have nothing significant to bring Him except willingness.

When Jesus entered the house, John leaped (though both babies were still developing in their mothers' wombs). Elizabeth also rejoiced that the Lord had come to her house. They could not know Jesus yet, but they were already rejoicing. A believer does not wait until they understand everything to celebrate Jesus. The more you know of Him, the more you celebrate Him.

Are you lacking joy in your life? Then maybe it has been a while since you saw something new in Jesus. The joy that baby Jesus brought while in the womb seemed minor to holding Him after He was born. A joyful life sees Jesus more and more.

If you think you have seen Jesus yet find that you still do not have joy, could it be that you are looking through dirty lenses or sepia-tinted filters? If your vision of Jesus is what you have seen in a hypocrite who claims to follow Jesus, you might dislike Him rather than rejoice. If you had an abusive parent or grandparent who made you go to church or quoted Bible verses to justify abuse, that filter could make you cringe from Jesus rather than leap for joy.

---

[72] See Luke 1:47.
[73] Luke 1:48, LITV.

Is your mental image of Jesus a red-faced screamer? A lazy, smelly person always looking for a handout? A deceptive money-taker? Your past experiences have handed you plenty of filters to see Jesus through. Will you throw them out and look with 20/20 vision, no props, no gimmicks?

Get back to the Scriptures. Get back to prayer. This is where we see Jesus. Remove the cage over your heart and remove any mask you have put on Him. Accept what Scripture says about Jesus. Have a "Let it be done to me according to your Word" kind of faith.

Seeing Jesus brings joy. As we go through this tour together, you will find moments of joy as your eyes open to Truth. Respond to that—give voice to it. God blessed Mary for this. Zachariah did not, however, and God silenced him. When the Lord opens your eyes, open your mouth. When the Spirit moves on you, speak. If we keep silent, we are not walking in simple faith like Mary.

When Mary opened her mouth and rejoiced in the Lord, she spoke to specific points of God's character.[74] If at times you find yourself without things to praise the Lord for, you can find all kinds of praising points in Mary's words. Here are some:

- God is my rescuer.
- He has done great things to me.
- His name is pure.
- He shows mercy to those who respect Him.
- He is strong and powerful.
- He knocked tough people off their thrones.
- He set up unknown people to take their places.
- He filled the hungry with good things.
- He drove out the rich with nothing.
- He helps His people.
- He keeps His promises.

---

[74] See Luke 1:49-55.

What can you say to Him to celebrate all that He is and honor His continual character qualities? Why not take a moment now and give your heart and voice to that?

Looking at Mary's physical experience, we pick up some spiritual clues. With Jesus "in" you, you talk differently. You see things through a new lens. When Jesus dwells within, you rejoice and bring joy and blessing to others. Want a fulfilling life that touches others? Make sure Jesus lives "in" you.

Elizabeth set a good example by accepting God as doing the impossible, and she responded with maturity to this young woman's pregnancy. Liz waited for the better part of a century to conceive a child. She could easily have been jealous of the girl who got to birth the Messiah.

Those who walk by faith and accept God's plan for their lives do not need to envy those who have different roles. Find your place and settle yourself into doing what the Lord has empowered you for. Jesus's people shouldn't compete with each other. Elizabeth not only recognized the greater role Mary had but rejoiced with her in it.

My grandmother served in a useful role in the lives of others, but I never heard her talk about being a "minister" or complaining she didn't have someone else's ministry. One of her skills was food. She fed people at camp meetings and church dinners. She baked and decorated birthday cakes and stocked them in a freezer so that all the children in the church would have something special for their birthdays. She was constantly doing something for others, and she did an excellent job of stocking, planning, and serving. You will find fulfillment when you find your place with Jesus and do what He has given you to do!

Like Mary, our attitude should be: "I am nothing exceptional!"[75] She was a humble young woman. She told both the angel and Liz that she was just a slave of the Lord—nothing special.[76] Elizabeth exhibited the same humility—"Who am I to meet with the mother of my Lord?"[77] Here is the key to getting close to Jesus—a humble heart.

---

[75] See Luke 1:48.
[76] See Luke 1:38, 48.
[77] See Luke 1:43.

PASS ON THE VISION

THE MIRACLE HAPPENED in Zachariah's house. It appears that shortly after Mary headed home, Elizabeth had her boy.[78] She had celebrated with Mary, and now others came and celebrated with her. Be an Elizabeth to someone. Join in someone else's joy; others will rejoice with you.

Zack and Liz's late-in-life "surprise" has been born. Liz's "neighbors and her relatives heard that the Lord magnified His mercy with her"[79] and came rejoicing. In the last chapter, we saw Mary magnify the Lord by praising Him. Toward us, He magnifies good things. He could magnify judgment and one day will, but right now He has zoomed His focus on being merciful toward us, allowing us to see Jesus.

How did the Lord enlarge mercy to Liz? Finally giving her a child seems merciful enough. He showed excessive generosity by giving her the son who would prepare the way for Him to come to earth. Have you ever felt like you are behind others, like you were late to bloom in some areas? God hasn't lost His magnifying glass. Stay faithful. When ready, He will complete your purpose, and you will find it a lot bigger than just keeping up with everyone else.

---

[78] See Luke 1:56-57.
[79] Luke 1:58, LITV.

51

How does a miracle like this happen? Zack and Liz did not believe a child into existence. It happened because God promised and they believed. Though many today look at Jesus through a filter of "name it and claim it," Zack wouldn't claim it. Mary did not name and claim that she would have a virgin birth. Liz did not begin expecting a child until the Lord said she would have one.

Our faith comes by the word of the Lord,[80] not the word of our wishes. Abraham and Sarah did not name and claim Isaac into existence—they laughed when it seemed so overwhelming. Rather than I speak and expect the Lord to fulfill it, I want to hear Him speak and watch in faith as He fulfills it in me.

Too many times a person's miracle goes to his head and he forgets to honor the One who gave it to him. Don't let your miracle eclipse your obedience. At this point, Zachariah could have ignored God's command to name his son John. After all, who would know if he was disobeying? He was the only one present when Gabriel gave the orders. Zack learned a thing through his trial.

Since Zack couldn't speak for himself, helpful friends and relatives stepped right in. They decided to name the child after his daddy—Zachariah.[81] That's when mom stepped up and said, "No way. We are calling him John!"

But that made no sense to their social group. They knew Zachariah would not live forever and it would be nice to leave a son after him to carry on the same name as his daddy. Besides, no one in the family line had the name "John,"[82] and ancestral names meant a lot in those days.

---

[80] See Romans 10:17.
[81] See Luke 1:59.
[82] See Luke 1:61. While the name John, from Johanan, was not in their ancestry, there were several individuals named Johanan throughout Hebrew history such as one priest during Solomon's time in I Chronicles 6:9-10 and a prophet in Jeremiah 40.

These helpful people were not going to stop with the "Not so"[83] from Liz. They got Zack's attention and made signs to him what the name should be.[84] Obviously, he could not hear as well as not speak.[85]

Zack would not cave to this passive-aggressive bullying. When the Lord begins to move in your life, you experience a counter-pressure from the other side. This can come via opinions from friends or others whose approval you crave. A follower of Jesus must want His approval more than acceptance from peers or human idols.

To tell the others what the name of his son would be, Zachariah most likely wrote on a wooden tablet covered with wax. He scratched into the surface, "John is his name."[86]

Zack had moved forward as a man of faith. Mary exercised faith from the angel's first word. Zack learned that he did not have to understand to believe. Because of his faith, his voice came back. Miracles happen for those who believe, even if some of us take a while to get it.

When Zack believed, "Immediately his mouth was opened and his tongue loosed, and he spoke, praising God."[87] If someone has a problem praising God, it often reveals a faith issue. As you see Him better, your mouth will want to respond. Let that happen!

This miracle sparks wonder throughout the neighborhood.[88] With John's arrival grabbing so much attention, one wonders what will the next child be like. This primes the reader up for the arrival of Jesus. John would only give the

---

[83] Luke 1:60, LITV.
[84] See Luke 1:62.
[85] In Luke 1:20, the word translated "mute" or "dumb" previously could also apply to a person who could not hear or speak.
[86] Luke 1:63, LITV.
[87] Luke 1:64, NKJV.
[88] See Luke 1:65-66.

opening act in front of the red curtain. The main show is coming soon!

As Zachariah praised the Lord, the Spirit filled him. Prophets of old, including Moses and the elders of Israel, also experienced the power of the Spirit causing them to speak God-given words. He still does this today.

Zack made up for his year of silence. The Spirit of prophecy caused him to tell of the work of God to save His people.[89] Repeated references to salvation, redemption, and deliverance pepper his monologue of hope.[90] Zack points out that God's prophets had declared this coming salvation since the dawn of time.

Manmade traditions and religious filters have distorted another part of the Jesus story, the word "saved." This word carries the idea of being rescued out of harm's way or delivered from impending destruction by malicious forces. Jews were looking for salvation from their enemy oppressors. Like Israel today, they simply wanted to be preserved.

What they understood about salvation and what Christians should believe about it will come together in an amazing way at the end of this book series. For years I read these verses and themes over and over, but only once I got the Gospels in full view did I understand this topic fully. We are getting there!

Zack first speaks of Jesus. He declares how the God of Israel "visited and worked redemption for His people."[91] Like a bull tossing an attacker with his horns, so the Lord comes to defend and protect His people. We know Zack spoke of Jesus here because he speaks of this Man arriving from within the

[89] See Luke 1:67.
[90] See Luke 1:68-75.
[91] Luke 1:68, LITV.

"house" of David the king, which Jews would have recognized as being the Messiah.[92]

But how does the coming of Jesus apply to you and me? I have not found a connection to Jewish ancestry in my Scandinavian ancestors. This prophecy is much broader than one race threatened by militant neighbors.

Some people do not seek Jesus because they do not realize they have dangerous enemies. Seeing our enemy better will help awaken the desire to see Jesus. Let's examine that thought, next.

---

[92] See Luke 1:69. And this certainly is not about John, who comes from the priestly line of his parents.

SEEING IN DARKNESS?

I WALKED INTO MY KITCHEN this morning and fumbled around in the darkness to find something. I could not see it. (No, this is not a story of breaking my little toe.) I flipped on the light switch over the kitchen sink and a bunch of stuff instantly appeared before me. Some things had been sitting on the window sill and a few on the counter—but the darkness made it seem nothing was there at all.

I live in the country where nighttime comes with industrial-strength darkness. At my house, I can see many more stars in the night sky than I can in the city. Stars pop out at us from millions of miles and light-years away; the light still penetrates, and the darkness cannot stop it. True Light works this way. Born in darkness, none of us see Jesus, to begin with.

Darkness has flooded the world, spiritually. Before we can move forward with this amazing production, we must first embrace a fact: without Jesus, even the best people live in darkness. They will continue to stub their toes on the cabinets and corners of human experience unless they find the Light. Humans do not "find their own light" or became illumined by self-contemplation or sophisticated logic.

Some religious ideologues treat Christianity as education or informational enlightenment. We will not "arrive" by attaining a religious group's special knowledge or copyrighted insights about Jesus. What happened to seeing and knowing Him as real, personal, friend? We only want to see the Jesus the Scriptures promise us.

"In the beginning, God created the heavens and the earth."[93] We've all experienced an "in the beginning" though those early details escape us—development in the womb, birth, crawling—yet we don't remember those things.

John's Gospel also begins, "In the beginning." The whole book builds on themes of creation: light, spoken word, breath of life, image of God, and more. In our Creator "was life, and the life was the light of men."[94]

In the beginning, the Creator spoke light into existence. And boom! It was instant. First, He created earth and sky, but darkness covered the planet. When He spoke, the light chased away the darkness.

Without light, plants would die on our planet, animals would starve, and all life would cease. Although sunlight still washes our planet, it flounders in spiritual darkness. Those not in the light fumble around, like me in the kitchen.

They cannot see Jesus even though we can easily reach Him. A spirit of darkness blinds people from seeing Jesus. Not only can they not see the hope in this life, but they also do not sense the danger.

I have known the Jesus accounts my whole life—His name is one of the first words I said. As a child, He dynamically and memorably filled me with His Spirit. Yet, only decades later did I begin to see Him. Before that, in spite of all the experiences—and they were legit—I did not let his light penetrate me so I could see.

---

[93] Genesis 1:1, LITV.
[94] John 1:4, LITV.

The more I see Him, the better I see me. The Light enhances how I see life.

You might assume that this journey concerns finding better information. No. We are talking about illumination. Academies and institutions can provide more information. Jesus, the Light, alone gives illumination.

You will see that Jesus does not illuminate with facts and statistics. In fact, He has an art form of helping people become more aware of their darkness so they can see the Light better. That Light helps us see life and its meaning.

Humanity's first enemy appeared in the middle of God's perfect scene on earth: the beautiful and fruitful garden. We see the first hint of the devil and his forces in the Gospels when John says, "Light shines in the darkness."[95] Our enemies exist in the unseen realm.

Demonic power destroys many people, and can even destroy unfocused Christians. Unaware of the darkness, they learn how to navigate in the dark, not knowing what they are missing. By seeing Jesus, we overcome that darkness. "The light shines in the darkness, and the darkness did not overtake it."[96]

Being aware of our enemy, we realize our need for rescue. Jesus (meaning 'the-God-who-saves') comes to deliver us "from the hand of all the ones hostile to us."[97] Through Him, we break the forces of darkness, have peace in our homes, and get free from the captivity of the evil one.

The prophets told about this rescue operation long before it finally happened.[98] They told us we would be "delivered out of

---

[95] John 1:5, LITV.
[96] John 1:5, LITV.
[97] Luke 1:71, LITV.
[98] See Luke 1:72-73.

the hand of those hostile to us" so we could "serve Him without fear, in consecration and righteousness before Him all the days of our life."[99]

God desires to free you. He holds a specific plan for your life in His impossible mission. Observe the paradox in modern Christianity. "Believers" have misunderstood the message and do not see Jesus correctly. Thus, they are neither free from the enemy nor able to fulfill their purpose in life. This low living gives a bad reputation to the words "Christian" and "Jesus."

Life is more than living your own dreams. Every non-Christian tries to find meaning and life-purpose. Only through Jesus and following His Way can people become unchained from what the enemy clamped onto them. Only by grasping and applying the details of the Gospel can you or I transform into that person of purity and purpose He designed us to be.

Could you pause for a moment and accept God's plan in your life? We will understand it better soon, but let's commit now to access all that He came for.

Now that we have looked at words from the Gospel of John, let's look again at the life of the other John. After declaring the role of Jesus, Zachariah spoke into his own son's life, giving him an outline for his future ministry.[100] He would bulldoze the path for the highest Being ("the Most High"[101]).

John would not grow up to be the young man flipping burgers, gaming himself to sleep, chasing wild girls, and just trying to figure out life. He did not have to wonder about what to do with his life. He grew up with a father speaking life-purpose into his spirit.

---

[99] Luke 1:74-75, LITV.
[100] See Luke 1:76-79.
[101] Luke 1:76, LITV.

The ministry of Jesus would springboard off John's preparation. Likewise, John's ministry launched from Zachariah's foundation. Today, too many fathers and mothers speak hatred, frustration, and selfishness into their children's lives. As John experienced, a boy today needs a man speaking into his life with purpose, values, and meaning for existence. Like Zachariah, many godly men could speak into a young person's life.

Liz did this for Mary, too. It does not take wealth or great education to believe in a person. Listen to their dreams and desires. Speak encouragement.

This need for multi-generational vision is not a new thing: it's basic to humanity. In Genesis, a "genealogy" or family history tells the adventures of sons who kept their fathers' names alive.[102] The accomplishment of the sons serves as the story of each father. Next, the ultimate Son comes to complete the story of the ultimate Father.

John will grow up to have his life focused on the coming of Jesus, the face of the Lord.[103] Zachariah's prophecy gives us an early glimpse of Jesus:

1. He rescues us by pardoning us from sin.[104] Our sins gave the enemy access to our lives. By taking away our sins, the evil forces' rights of access fall away, too.
2. God's mercy comes from His "tender heart"[105] toward those whom the evil one victimized.
3. Jesus is the Dayspring.[106] This refers to the sun that springs up in the East, chasing away darkness as it

---

[102] For example, the record of Jacob's story is the life of Joseph, beginning in Genesis 37:2. The sons, descendants, made the father's story. See also Gen. 5:1; 11:27; 25:19. The life of the Son of God shows the world what the Father is like. Our lives tell the world about our Father.
[103] See Luke 1:76, LITV with Malachi 3:1 and II Corinthians 4:6.
[104] See Luke 1:77.
[105] Luke 1:78, LITV.
[106] See Luke 1:78.

brings light to the day. He rises in your life, piercing your darkness. You sense this even as we take these moments to focus on Him.

4. He appears to those sitting in darkness and shadowed by death.[107] Being alone in the dark paralyzes you because you don't know what will hit you next. You cannot move forward freely or accomplish anything worthwhile. To us, trapped in meaninglessness and confusion from the enemy, He comes to give clarity.

5. This Man comes "to direct our feet into the way of peace."[108] Anyone who struggles to look for direction in life will find clarity and focus in Jesus. You don't need to scramble, trying to ladder climb your way to the top. This restful sense of purpose will not depend on your performance.

All this and more is coming, and we have hardly begun!

Life flows from our Creator.[109] Without Him, we are "dead." As we experience more and more of His Life, no matter how religious we've been, we will see everything in a whole new Light.

I only ask you to keep your eyes open. As you read each verse, each time you glimpse Him, as you talk to Him, let Him do that work inside you. I cannot do it for anyone. I can only point out the sunrise to a friend, not create it. I can point out what I've seen of Jesus; the rest is up to you. And Him.

Several years ago, I fell into a dead zone. My marriage was rough. I had strained my relationship with my children. My motivations for life disappeared. Through all that, I still did all the church stuff, yet I was dead.

---

[107] See Luke 1:79.
[108] Luke 1:79, LITV.
[109] See John 1:4.

There was no funeral because I did not know I had died. I did not smell the decay because I had not gotten downwind of my carcass. This all happened years after my dramatic experience alone in prayer. I was "saved, sanctified, and filled with the Holy Ghost," as they say, but I was not seeing as I should.

Dead religion and Christian hypocrites develop when people get their eyes off Jesus. Some churches focus on their buildings or their programs. Someone may have once seen Jesus but later got his or her eyes on possessions He provided rather than Him.

Today, many talk "Jesus" but have no life. They drop that word but have dropped The Word. Their lives meander in the dark—not finding the light.

I wish I could explain exactly what changed in me. I wish I could give you a simple three-step solution. Your seeing Jesus will proceed according to your own uniqueness and originality.

Only when I began to see Jesus new and fresh again, did I truly come to life. Finally, the Light broke through my darkness. Now that I have found a dynamic friendship with Jesus, I live in a whole new world.

Every day of our lives should focus on Jesus. Seeing Jesus is a process, not an event. The more Light around you, the better you see everything else.

What you see of Jesus you will not be able to keep to yourself. When you see a beautiful scene, like a stunning purple sunset or a tree sparkling with ice crystals, you want to share it with others. So, be ready to tell others when you see Jesus in ways you never have before. That jaw-dropping kind of experience inspired what we look at next.

JESUS CHANGES OUR MORALS

MARY WALKED HOME from Elizabeth's and by that point might have been showing her baby bump. Her fiancé Joseph had to work through a little trauma when he heard she was pregnant. He only believed half her story: that she was expecting. The part about the Spirit causing the conception, though? He wasn't buying it.

Let's be serious here. Would you have believed her? The Scripture states clearly that not only was she a virgin but that she conceived "before they came together."[110] You know what this looked like to everyone else.

Not wanting to be married to an unfaithful woman, as he thought she was, Joe made plans to break the covenant of marriage they had already entered.[111] In their legal system, this was divorce. He still loved her and did not want her shamed or punished (as they typically would do to teach others a lesson). Here we see Joseph's tender heart along with his commitment to moral purity. The honorable character of both mother and father sets an example for us today.

---

[110] Matthew 1:18, NKJV.
[111] See Matthew 1:19.

The angel of the Lord appeared to Joseph in a dream. The heavenly being told him not to fear taking Mary in marriage because her baby was "generated by the Holy Spirit."[112] She had not been messing around.

When Joseph heard from heaven, he decided to not break it off but to follow through with Mary being his wife. Please allow me a soapbox moment. Before anyone gets married, they should hear from heaven, too. [Gets off soapbox.]

This new info Joseph learned about the pregnancy brought a whole new set of concerns... and hopes. Before Joseph could see Jesus, he had to be willing to take ridicule and rejection. To those who knew Joseph, it looked like Mary had been unfaithful. Others assumed the two of them had been sleeping together before their wedding.[113] Either way, people were going to talk.

Some people don't see Jesus because they are not willing to endure some embarrassment they don't deserve. Joseph could have walked off and let some other guy marry her. In many societies, taking a stand for Jesus means being excluded or mocked. Imagine what Joe faced.

"Dad, I decided to go through with the wedding."

"Marry whom?"

"Mary."

"You said she was pregnant. You were going to break it off, right? You'll destroy your reputation."

---

[112] Matthew 1:20, LITV.

[113] Speaking of the marriage covenant they had then is a little difficult because our modern methods are quite different. Their marriages would begin legally before they actually moved in together. The wedding celebration that we think of would come the week they became physically one. However, their commitment to each other had already been legally struck, which is why he would have to divorce her before they had even had a wedding, as we think of it.

"She's a good girl, dad. Her baby is from God."

"Joe..." awkward pause. "What are you talking about, son? That's the dumbest thing I've ever heard."

For Joseph to see Jesus, he had to obey. He had received a word from God that came while he slept. No one else had heard of such a thing as a virgin having a baby.[114] It takes great faith to rewrite your life because of something God said. To see Jesus clearly, we must willingly obey His words.

The angel's voice filled Joe's thoughts like it had Zack's. He received a command to name his Son, as well. "You will call Him Jesus." The name matters! The purpose of Jesus coming was salvation: "Yahweh-Saves" or "the God who saves" will rescue His people from their sins![115]

Further, Joseph discovers Jesus's true identity as "God with us!"[116] I believe Joseph was in shock while hearing all of this. The reality of it all does not hit him until later, as we will see.

In a new way, now, Joseph's character proves him exemplary in every way. Joseph and Mary begin married life together.[117] Then, they did a shocking thing: he "did not know her until she bore her son, the First-born."[118]

---

[114] The original prophecy in Isaiah 7:14 came in Hebrew, in which the word for young woman (*'almâh*) could mean a virgin or even a young married woman. Jewish hearers might not have taken it to mean a literal virgin. Septuagint (Greek versions of the OT) did use the term specific to a virgin, so there was that. When Luke and Matthew confirmed that this applied to a physically intact virgin (*parthenos*) we had a solid case of what that prophecy meant.
[115] See Matthew 1:21.
[116] Matthew 1:23, LITV.
[117] See Matthew 1:24.
[118] Matthew 1:25, LITV. Jesus is called Mary's firstborn, but God's only-born.

Did you catch that? Joe did not sleep with her until after the baby was born. Why would any newlywed man put off the honeymoon for six months? Because Joseph and Mary knew the Scriptures.

The prophet did not say a virgin would only conceive but that the virgin would give birth. If she was not a virgin at the time of delivery, they would have violated God's promises. In other words, because of Jesus, these two restrained their human desires.

These are the first followers, also known as disciples, of Jesus. Already this Man is shaping lives, and He is only in His second trimester. Already He was moving feet away from rebellion and onto the path of peace![119]

I'm thankful for having godly parents who understood these biblical values. Although I was exposed to and involved in things I wish now I had never seen as a child, I am thankful the Lord kept me through all those years. My wife kept her virginity for marriage, and by the strength of the Lord, we defied the odds by keeping ourselves for one another until after marriage.

In North American culture, 80% of young people have given in to sexual involvement before adulthood. Even among Christian denominations, the same numbers emerge. We are looking through a dirty lens if it is abnormal for a girl to still be a virgin when she marries. Jesus's biography began with a person of purity; such an accomplishment should not be rare now among those who claim Him.

At the same time, it would be wrong to shame those who have sinned sexually in the past. God's grace includes them. Too many girls give in to sexual advances because they are afraid that if they turn a guy down, they will lose him. That is the guy she needs to lose. I want to ask such a girl, "If he will not respect your sexuality before marriage, will he respect another woman's after

[119] See Luke 1:79.

marrying you?" God can do so much more in our lives when we put Him first in areas like this.

To keep your sexual purity, put Jesus first. Next, set boundaries. Jews in that day did not believe in men being alone with women other than immediate family.

A similar safeguard is wise today. Physical contact early in a relationship could lead to sexual contact before marriage. Intimate involvement drugs a person's mind to not be able to reason and assess if you would be compatible lifetime partners.

We must dedicate our homes/families to purity. We cannot raise kids who choose godly mates based on the right values if they keep seeing godless heroes. TV romances are not real life, and they set young people up for a broken one. If looks are not everything, shouldn't we fall in love with character and godliness? Are there any shows or movies emphasizing the importance of a humble spirit?

Joseph and Mary retained sexual self-control because they knew marriage was not about them. Marriage is before the Lord. These young people might have been 15 and 19 years old, a time when hormones drive strongest.[120] But those who live for Jesus live differently. Mary and Joseph give silent witness to the fact that self-control is possible for those devoted to Jesus because "nothing is impossible!"

Are you rebuilding after sexual shame? Determine that your past will not define your future. Find hope in seeing Jesus. If He can keep a person from falling into those pits of regret, He is just as strong to pull one out of them. These are the kinds of chains of darkness[121] He came to free us from. Keep looking to the Light; your path of peace is coming. When you have

---

[120] The term used to describe young Mary indicates her age rage. Many young men married around 19-20 years old.
[121] See Luke 1:79.

recovered, help warn other travelers that "the bridge is out ahead" on the road to sexual self-indulgence.

In celebrating the strength of character Jesus inspired in Mary and Joseph, I want to be careful to not give the wrong impression either. Some of us had things happen to us beyond our control. Magazines, dirty-minded friends, porn videos, evil games, and a host of other dangers make it tough for a child to grow up with a pure body, let alone mind. Perhaps you were the victim or were under-informed about what was happening when someone led you down the wrong path.

Have you ever wondered what your life would be like if those things hadn't happened to you? I have, too. I wanted to go back and rewrite those low moments of my past.

In the next chapter, we begin looking at something that gives me hope in spite of all the scars and shame. Did you know a pleasant surprise hides among those unwelcome moments of life? Look with me at how Jesus takes even those uncomfortable situations that were out of our control and makes them meaningful.

UNWELCOME CIRCUMSTANCES

O NE DAY, a farmer's horse escaped from his field and ran into the hills. His neighbors told him what a shame it was, saying, "Sorry about your bad luck."

"Good luck, bad luck, who knows?" the man said.

The next week, the horse came back, leading a few wild horses onto the farmer's property. The neighbors now told him how great this was and expressed how fortunate he had been.

"Good luck, bad luck, who knows?" the man said.

Later, the farmer's son fell off the back of one of the wild horses while training it and broke his leg. "That's very bad luck," the onlookers said.

"Good luck, bad luck, who knows?" the man said.

A few weeks later, the army came into the village and forced all the young men to march into battle. They rejected the farmer's son because of his broken leg.

Good luck?

Bad luck?

Who knows?[122]

Unexpected events happen and sometimes it feels like there is no meaning or purpose to what happens. Regardless of our circumstances, we get to choose the attitude and response we will have to those events. Have you had one of those "where is God in this mess?" kind of moments? Sometimes those "messes" put us directly in line with God's will for our lives.

Pregnant for the first time, Mary felt like her intestines had smashed into her lungs. Her skin felt stretched like a balloon (if only she had known what one was). Then, she receives word that she and Joseph had to travel something like ninety miles south to Bethlehem in Judea.

Some big-wig politician up in Washin—er, Rome—said they had to answer to a census. Easy for him to say, but not easy on this youngster toting a baby in her belly. The trip home from Liz's house in the hill country of Judea back to Nazareth did not wear her down so badly when she was three months along. She had not planned on crunching gravel underfoot for several days at the end of her third trimester.

In order to see Jesus, Mary had to walk with the Lord into the unknown. She did not know what life would be like in Nazareth. She did not know if she would have the Baby on the trip there or arrive in Bethlehem first.

We say we want to see Jesus; are we willing to journey into the unknown? Are you reading this book because you want something to confirm your religious beliefs or because you are willing to take a path no one else does? If it is the way of the Lord, will you walk it no matter how long the journey? Will you pursue His plan even when you don't know when your moment of clarity will come?

---

[122] This version of the tale was adapted from Sadhana De Mello, *A Way to God*, (St. Louis, MO: Institute of Jesuit Sources, 1979), 134.

When the couple arrived at Joseph's family's home in Bethlehem, there were more surprises. Since Joseph's family was from this area, Joe and Mary most likely went to stay with relatives in the family home. Apparently, Joseph and Mary were not the only ones who came in from out of town. When they arrived, the spare room was already taken.[123] They couldn't even find space enough for an inflatable mattress in the living room. Not that she wanted to have a baby there anyway.

Good luck? Bad luck? Who knows?

It appears to be bad luck. Why taxation now? Why no private place for giving birth to a baby? Where will the baby rest? Why such stinky accommodations? Mary had been a good girl; she didn't deserve this. God uses things in our lives that "just so happen."

Scrolling back through the old tweets, we discover that the divine plan had always been for the child to be birthed in Bethlehem. The Lord told Bethlehem that "out of you He shall come forth to Me to become One ruling in Israel; and His goings forth have been from of old, from the days of eternity."[124] The Word would show up in that little hood!

What a coincidence that they would be in Bethlehem when the baby was born. How random that a Roman politician would require them to travel. If life had not gone chaotic, the promised Child would have been born in Nazareth. That would not have fulfilled what was appointed for Him. Yes, that uncomfortable journey and the miserable conditions of nesting among the animals put them directly in the will of God.

Why would family members put them out in the cold like this? Think about it. They had been together for six months and

---

[123] The word translated "inn" (*kataluma*) is possibly not an inn but a spare room. In Luke 22:11, Jesus and the disciples were not eating in an inn, but in a spare room (*kataluma*) or upper room, where arrangements had been made for them.

[124] Micah 5:2, LITV; See also John 7:42.

she was now nine months pregnant. His fam did the math. Joseph's mom was probably like, "That girl can just sleep with the animals if she wants to live like one." There's no telling what she thought, but the awkwardness of the surroundings tell us that Mary's world was in turmoil.

Perhaps Mary birthed baby Jesus in a cave as one tradition suggests. It could very well be she was in the outdoors in an open courtyard in front of the house if the family had no room for them inside. Or, in the case of a poor home with no courtyard, they most likely stayed in the same lower room where a few animals were kept. Whew! What aromatherapy!

In pain, afraid, feeling very alone, she saw Jesus for the first time. We want to see Him on the sunny days from our comfy chair on the front porch while the birds sing. Those dark nights though, those places where you feel so out of place, that time in your life where your mind screams, "What is going on here?!" That's where you learn to hold Him close. The Jesus you find in your pain becomes more than a picture on the wall or a story in a book.

You don't have to play the victim of unwelcome circumstances to find Him, but we do have to take the forgotten path. We have to be willing to go to the place of humility where He will be born in us. Everything in us wants to fight the chaos and command the unpredictability of life, but Jesus still shows up in the most disjointed times of our lives.

Maybe you picked up this book to find a quick and easy way to see Jesus. Remember, how Mary first found Him. Somehow He seems to enter the barns of our lives more often than the fancy gates of palaces where life seems happily ever after.

My germ alarm screams at the thought of a baby born near animals. When was that area last pressure washed? Did they disinfect everything? Did Joseph help Mary with breathing techniques or was he passed out in a trauma-induced coma? Did anyone help her while she was having the Baby? She had to wrap Him up herself. Where did you go, Joe?

She bundled Him up with strips of cloth. Where did those come from? Were they intended for use on the animals? Some say that is how they wrapped up lambs that would be used for Temple sacrifices. How fitting.

Are you willing to do what it takes to see Jesus even if no one else joins you in this? Her labor and travail in childbirth probably lasted a few hours. Then its pain gave way to joy, darkness surrendered to the Light. Once you break past the obstacles, the distractions, the struggles, the blinding pains of life, seeing Jesus will make it all worth it. Once He is right there with you, all those things become distant memories.

After the Baby was all bundled up snug and sleeping happily, maybe she paused to think. Why had she come here to this unfamiliar and unwelcoming city of David? She could have stayed in Nazareth—Joseph could have taken care of the census and tax stuff without her. Maybe she wanted to get away from the accusing stares from family back home. Everyone assumed she had done the naughty thing. Treatment wasn't much better here, but at least she had her man. Maybe she couldn't explain even to herself why she was there.

Was this coincidence?

The word "coincident" comes from two Latin words "to fall" and "together." Sometimes when things look like they are falling apart, they actually are falling together if we keep Jesus at the center of the scene. We cannot control the random events of life, but we can control our response. Looking at Jesus will make it all worth it—no matter how out of place we may be.

It just so happened that there was a census. It just so happened that Joseph's family was from the town where the Messiah was to be born. It just so happened he had to go there right before the birth. It just so happened that your world turned upside down, too.

Looking at this journey, it does my heart good to see that God used a godless government to orchestrate His plan written down ages before. I don't have to worry about world events or situations out of my control. He knows what He is doing and if I hold Jesus close, it will all fall together according to His plan.

One night there was a terrible storm that came through a city near where we live. This massive tornado claimed the lives of dozens of victims. The night this happened, my family and I drove up to help friends from our church who had found two of their relatives that had died from the storm.

We became overwhelmed trying to drive across the city while avoiding debris in the road. We had to stop to change a punctured tire and struggled to find our way with many buildings and landmarks totally gone. Cell phone service was either down with the mangled towers or so jammed that even texts would hardly go through.

After trying to drive around to check on another lady from our church, we managed to make it to the hospital to try to find the grieving family whose surviving nephew was facing surgery because of injury from the storm. Inside, the hospital scene took me by surprise. Wounded people stood around everywhere in blue gowns. The staff members of the overcrowded ER were dealing with life-threatening emergencies first.

Right as I walked in the doors, I spotted a man I knew among the wounded and disheveled survivors. I did not know he was in town, so I did not think to look him up after the storm. He was in great pain having gone through the tornado in his car while his windows shattered around him. We prayed together and Jesus instantly lifted the pain from his body. He contacted us a few days later still in awe of how miraculously the Lord touched him that night.

Searching for our other friends proved unsuccessful. Frustrated, we went outside and managed to get a call through. They had already driven home, leaving one family member to ride in the helicopter with the boy who would be airlifted to another hospital. Our family loaded up and headed that direction. I felt unsettled as if we had not done much good for anyone in that mess.

On our way out of the parking lot, we spotted a woman crossing the street. Knowing it was a long walk from there to anywhere with limited street lights, my wife and I agreed to offer her a ride. Pulling up to the curb, we were shocked to see the woman from the family we were looking for. She did not get to travel in the helicopter, not realizing her husband had already headed home. Unable to connect on the phone, she decided to walk the 20 or so miles home, for lack of a better plan.

Looking back, was it a coincidence that put us in the path of a man right when he needed prayer? We "just so happened" to meet up with our abandoned friend as she began her journey and were able to drive her to meet up with her family. I'm not sure any of that lessened the grief and trauma of that evening. Still, we got a startling reminder of how the Lord can make chaotic circumstances fall together when we least expect it.

Perhaps something you thought happened to ruin your life becomes what saves it. God showed up on this planet as a little baby in perfect timing and perfect location.[125] Yet the whole series of events looked like a disaster to Mary. What you might think is a black hole could become a finely ordered universe God has structured for your destiny. You will impact many lives by how you respond to your surroundings.

What upsets have you seen in life? What disturbing and annoying circumstances are you in right now? Where might the Lord be at work in your frustration? Determine now that He will

---

[125] See Galatians 4:4.

get glory out of this. Jesus will show up in your crazy, awkward life and make good of it.[126]

---

[126] See Romans 8:28.

CELEBRATE THE SURPRISE

HAVE YOU EVER FELT like a misfit or an outcast?

Shepherds in the first century did not have the best of reputations. They were on the low end of society. Many had a problem confusing "yours" and "ours" as they roamed the countryside, taking what wasn't theirs at times.[127] When the flocks of sheep came by your town, you might double-check that you had latched all the doors tightly.

You can't imagine God would have anything to do with such roaming characters. Maybe He didn't care what other people thought about them. For these unnamed men and women on the Bethlehem countryside, He decided to put on a show.[128] After all, God has a history of putting shepherds in His family of redemption: Abraham, Jacob, Rachel, Moses, Zipporah, and David for example.

For lambs to be acceptable sacrifices at the Temple, they had to grow up in the wilderness. Sheep raised between Bethlehem and Jerusalem generally would become sacrifices. These shepherds must have been watching lambs dedicated to

---

[127] Morris, *Luke*, TNTC 3.
[128] See Luke 2:8.

the Lord. He then invited them to see another Lamb who would be the ultimate sacrifice.

Speaking of unexpected events, imagine a shining angel showing up in the darkness of night.[129] That would have terrified me as it did them. First, he told them to listen up and chill.[130] Then, he told them to celebrate!

The Lord had arranged for this moment for thousands of years. Yet the humans in town were sleeping through it. Scholars and religious devotees a few miles away in Jerusalem also missed the moment.

People have let you down before. Think about God's disappointment. He had invited people to this surprise party for years and no one showed. What would you do? Go invite a bunch of people to blow the party horns and eat the cake and candies with you? He did. The shepherds weren't watching for this moment, but they weren't so busy with sheep that they couldn't take some time out to congratulate the new parents.

When the angel announced the birth of Jesus, he called Him the Savior.[131] Even the not-so-spiritual shepherds would have found this surprising. To the Jewish mind, the only Savior is God.[132] Over the noise of bleating sheep, the workers heard the angel tell them that God had been born in Bethlehem among the animals.[133]

This truth fills in a theological misunderstanding. Many Jews had adopted a view of the Christ (Messiah, Chosen One) that He would be a powerful king like David. The angel tells the

---

[129] See Luke 2:9.
[130] See Luke 2:10.
[131] See Luke 2:11.
[132] See Luke 1:46 where Mary calls Him, "God my Savior." Hebrew passages referencing God as Savior include Isaiah 43:3, 11; 45:15, 21; 49:26; 60:16.
[133] See Luke 2:12.

back-woodsy shepherds that this Baby is the anointed Lord, Savior, God.

Heaven cannot contain the excitement. Many more angels appear and begin heralding this amazing impossibility. Standing in open fields where sheep chewed their cud and breathed steam into the chilly night air, the shepherds enjoyed the worship team from heaven.[134]

Whatever happened that night brought heaven and earth together. Never had such contagious excitement stirred in heaven and earth. The angels captured the wonder of the moment. The glorious God, high above all creation, had come down to earth, bringing a reason for happiness in the bleak and confusing life we call human.

Notice how the highest praises unto the Lord preceded their seeing Jesus. If a person struggles to see Jesus, praise and worship will help clear the skies. Have you ever wondered why churches and Christian media include so much singing? We got that idea from heaven. Songs and melodies of worship began there,[135] and we have learned that if we want heaven on earth, singing to the Lord about His power helps us enter that realm. When we offer heartfelt worship (not the performance style or showy kind of singing) the more we see Him.

This great joy comes to all people. For many in Israel, that surprised them. Many Jews thought God chose them above other races, rather than among them (as He selected Mary from among women).[136] The promise of great joy includes them and all tribes of the earth.

---

[134] See Luke 2:13. Of course, the text does not say they sang, but the words they said appear to be in metered verse, so it is likely they did sing these words. Similar instances appear in other heavenly passages where the words appear as poetry and likely were sung.

[135] See Job 38:7.

[136] See Luke 2:14.

Bringing heaven to earth still follows the same process: give glory to God in the highest. When we talk or sing about the Lord's greatness, we bring His peace and favor to humanity. Want a home filled with His presence? Rejoice that God our Savior has become human.

Hearing from heaven, a sense of urgency overwhelmed those country folk to respond to their sudden assignment. Why them? Why such common people? Why anyone? Perhaps the Lord likes to involve humans in what He is doing. Perhaps He just loves to spread joy to others.

To see Jesus, the shepherds had to give up sleep and put their possessions (the sheep) at risk. They left the familiar behind to go see something that did not make any sense, a Baby in a feed trough.[137] They saw Jesus because they were looking for Him. So have you.

In a sense, these country folk became the first eyewitnesses and the first preachers of Jesus.[138] From the beginning, when someone sees Jesus, they have this impulse to tell others. It didn't take a seminary education for them to tell others what they saw. Even a new believer feels that drive to proclaim the message (preach) about Jesus.

Are you still running on the power and joy of your first encounter with Jesus? How does seeing more about Him keep you talking to others?

While the shepherds run out shouting this news to the sleepy little town, Mary takes it all in. While the Jesus inside her brought joy and hope for her future, she now has experienced the Lord in a new way. She must reflect on Jesus's new role in her life and ponder this growing relationship.[139]

---

[137] See Luke 2:15-16.
[138] See Luke 2:17-18.
[139] See Luke 2:19.

Sometimes Jesus tears up your world. You may have thought you had everything figured out, but then hurts and surprises leave you exhausted and unsure of what might happen next. Serving the Lord is not all angel choirs on the hillside. Some private moments with the Lord are better pondered than proclaimed. Mature believers know what the Lord has given to us to share with others and what He has given to us to hold close to our hearts.

Seeing Jesus inspires us to praise Him. The shepherds went back to their sheep while celebrating God Himself.[140] What has the Lord already shown you about Himself since you began this book? Have you celebrated that by telling Him? Have you thanked Him for it? How have you proclaimed your good news to others?

---

[140] See Luke 2:20.

GOD WITH US

THE ANGEL DROPPED a clue to Joseph before the Child's birth that He would be "God with us."[141] This phrase came from one of those early "leaks" of God's classified plans. Another leak of the identity of Jesus comes from the creation record in Genesis chapter 1, but most overlook it as just a nice story.

While enjoying the streaming footage from Luke and Matthew, don't forget John's skills with the still-shot. Zooming back to the beginning, John shows us, "In the beginning was the Word, and the Word was with God, and the Word was God."[142]

Using well-known terminology, John reveals Jesus to us in light of creation. Contemporary thinkers of his day understood this "Word" he referenced. Devout Jews often referred to the Creator as the "Word of the Lord," or simply "the Word."[143] Why? God spoke everything into existence. He made it all by His Word. Greek thinkers also referred to the "Word" as a key to the physical world (as examined in Appendix A: "Opening Word").

---

[141] See Matthew 1:23 and Isaiah 7:14.

[142] John 1:1, this quote from the 1769 *King James Version of the Holy Bible*, hereafter referred to as "KJV."

[143] The Psalms show God doing all things by His Word (33:6; 107:20; 147:15-19).

82

Does John's "Word" have meaning for us? For the Wall Street investor looking for the "word on the street"? For the farmer asking, "What's the good word for the day?" Might it even speak to those struggling to find meaning in the hood? Word!

Today, you could pull up to a drive-thru, talk through an outdoor microphone, and order fries and a burger. When you do, you expect the workers to follow your words and assemble your meal for you in minutes. We get frustrated if someone gives us pickles when we asked for none or gives us a diet drink when we asked for tea. We expect our words to accomplish something.

You might hire a home builder and talk about the things you want to see in the kitchen or living room. Soon, with a lot of money, those words become a physical reality.

Words have hurt you; words inspire you. Words are not magical things. They move what happens on a daily basis.

It's not hard then to imagine and believe that this Being in another realm and who is more powerful than any other force could speak and physical reality would respond. His orders are at least a thousand times greater than anything we've given at a drive-thru. The Word was not just spoken by God but was more a part of Him than my word if I say I like blue tile flooring in a kitchen or ketchup without mustard on my burger.

Let's say you want to build a dream home. After years of earning and saving, you scrape together all your money and go see an architect. You explain exactly what you are looking for. You want a master bedroom with its own bathroom, a hot tub room with its own bathroom, a large kitchen with its own bathroom, a huge living room with its own bathroom, a wrap-around porch with its own bathroom, a personal gym with its own bathroom, a walk-in closet with its own bathroom, and a spiral staircase—but with no bathroom of course. I'm sure life offers more than extra bathrooms, but that shows what I know about luxury.

After you finish spilling all your dreams and desires for this house, the architect draws up the design. Then you get the bill. That book of blueprints for your new home costs as much as you had saved. Now, you're broke.

That does not stop you. You invite friends over to see your new "house." You all sit around in the little living room of your old house and turn the pages for them, showing them everything in the blueprints. They ooh-and-ah and tell you how nice that will be.

Let's say you invited me over the day you showed off your design for your new home. Afterward, I told you, "Hey, I have saved up a lot of money and I want to build a house. Do you mind if I use your blueprint book to build mine?"

"Of course not," you say, "you are welcome to it." Meanwhile, you start saving up again to get the money you need to build your own. So, I go out and build my house using your blueprints and everyone loves it.

Ten years later, you strike it rich and have what you need to build your dream home. You take those old blueprints and see your dreams become reality at last. Then you invite all your friends over to your new address.

Partway through the tour, someone says, "Hey, this house reminds me of something..." Then they look at you and say, "Did you copy Daniel's house?"

"No," you explain. "He copied mine. I designed that blueprint with my house in mind. I let Daniel copy what was intended for me." See? Your house is the original even if it was not formed until later.

That is what happened with humanity.

God had a strategy to create humans. More than a scheme to admire them, He intended to be in community with them. He had a plan to become one with those humans.

John's Gospel throws back the drop cloth. He shows the devout Jews a new angle they had never seen of God: "the Word was made flesh, and dwelt among us."[144] God the Creator (Word) became human. John got to walk and talk with Him.

What just happened? Let's have a look. The Bible tells us that Jesus is the image of the invisible God and the firstborn of creation.[145] It also tells us the Creator patterned the first humans "in His image."[146]

Before creating anything else, God had the divine design in mind: a body for Himself.[147] This concept became the blueprint He used for making the human race. Although the first human named Adam came to life long before Jesus was born, Jesus retains the title "firstborn" because He is the original, the divine design through which all other created things come.

Let's paraphrase John for a moment and say, "In the beginning was the Blueprint, and the Blueprint was with God and the Blueprint was God." This would lead to the conclusion: "The Blueprint became a house." While that's a fun illustration, John 1:14 says that the Word who is God became flesh and He literally tented—or housed—Himself among us.

The humanity of Jesus is God's "house"—the body where the invisible One has become visible. Everything of earth history comes in focus through the Word. John's wide-angle lens shows us that this is not the story of only a Jewish Messiah, but of a Man key to the universal rescue operation. In this saga, God comes unto His own creation becoming part of it and transforms it into what He is. This is the epic of "God with us."

---

144 John 1:14, NKJV.
145 See Colossians 1:15.
146 See Genesis 1:27.
147 See Hebrews 10:5.

Being real flesh and bone, God-with-us had to be circumcised according to the covenant of Abraham.[148] No male would be accepted in Israel if he was not circumcised. God-made-flesh conformed to His own rules.

At His circumcision on the eighth day, Mary and Joseph called Him "Jesus"—at least that is what English Bibles say.[149] Why did the angel tell them to use this Name? Let's find out.

For one thing, Scripture gives us a hero of the faith named Joshua[150] to look up to. He loved to linger in the presence of the Lord at the Tent of Meeting in the wilderness. He was captain of the armies of Israel. Once a servant of Moses, Josh eventually took his place as the leader when the prophet died.

Old Josh brought the people into the Promised Land, leading them to victory in battle after battle. What an amazing role to play in God's Book! No wonder so many people name their sons after this man of courage, Joshua.

Another Joshua/Jeshua[151] stood in the presence of the Lord several centuries later. He served in the role of the high priest during the time of the rebuilding of the Temple. What an amazing time to be alive! A generation of people reentered the Promised Land because they chose to worship the true God. The Accuser attacked this Joshua, but the Lord vindicated His servant and gave him new robes.[152]

---

[148] See Luke 2:21.
[149] See Luke 1:31; 2:21.
[150] See Numbers 13:16.
[151] The spelling of Joshua changed over the years. When Joshua, captain of Israel is referenced in Nehemiah 8:17, the spelling is more like Jeshua, the same as that of Joshua (Jeshua) the high priest. Coming over to the Greek, this caused some confusion in the KJV when translators placed the name "Jesus" in Acts 7:45 and Hebrews 4:8 when it should have been "Joshua."
[152] Zechariah 3:1-10.

Joshua/Jeshua comes from two words: the name of God and the word meaning 'to save.' So, this name could be understood as 'the God who Saves.' In the last chapter, we looked at how the Baby was referred to as Savior and Christ the Lord. The Hebrew for "Savior" is *yasha*. The Hebrew word for "salvation" is *yeshua*.

Notice the difference between Jeshua and Yeshua. Experts dialogue on whether the Hebrew letter *yod* was originally pronounced as a "y" or "j." Lacking podcasts or other audio clips from that time, we may never be able to prove one way or another.

Letter pronunciations change by region and throughout time, such as the silent "h" in some areas and the vocalized "h" in others. Talking about these letters would be more fun if a big yellow bird or a cookie-eating monster were looking for foam letters Y and J. Lacking that kind of expert help here, we have to accept that the pronunciation of "j" and "y" have changed over the years.

Let's pause from seeing Jesus to talk about hearing "Jesus" for a moment. There has been a lot of dialogue and some confusion about whether the name in English should be "Jesus" or something else. I believe those who seek to call our Lord with the correct pronunciation of His name have right motives. I don't want to discourage or insult anyone who wants to do their best in speaking of our Lord.

We want to see through a pure lens, not a distorted filter. I say this as one who was once worried that I had to say the Name in authentic Hebrew to say it correctly. In my quest for saying the name properly, I found dozens of pronunciations for Jesus's name in Hebrew.[153] They all claimed to be correct. However, because of the traumatic history of the Hebrew language, we cannot even say with certainty how all the letters should be pronounced.

---

[153] Some include *Yashua, Yasha, Yesha, Yehoshua,* and so on.

In every language, there is an established, standardized way to say the Savior's name. In English, it is "Jesus." In Appendix B: "Say the Name," you can read a thorough explanation of why this is so.

Jesus is the only One who can rescue humanity. The power comes because of who that Man is, not because of special vocalization of His name. In the last book in this Gospel series, I will give more proof that the name Jesus serves as the correct English word to use for this Man. For now, I would not let those who push some specialized pronunciation to worry you as they did me. While it is not wrong to want to recapture the exact pronunciation of His name, this pursuit can become a divisive obsession, obscuring our view of Him.

Our focus should be to know Jesus personally. Since many boys were named Jesus in that day,[154] descriptive words accompany His Name to give more clarity. Thus we have compound titles such as "Lord Jesus," "Jesus Christ," "Jesus of Nazareth," and similar expressions. The angel announced Him to the shepherds without using His proper name; he said they should go see Christ, the Savior.

Think back to Joshua the leader and Joshua/Jeshua in the Temple. What good luck that a captain and high priest should have the name of the Messiah! Or was it a coincidence? Jesus is Captain of our salvation who leads the forces of heaven. Jesus is our High Priest who gives us access to the throne room. Was it random chance that Jesus ended up with a name meaning Yahweh-Savior? Of course not.

Remember, the angel said to name the child Jesus because He would SAVE His people from their sins.[155] Jesus rescues

---

[154] For example, there was a believer named Jesus as well who went by "Justus," in Colossians 4:11.
[155] See Matthew 1:21.

humanity, this is core to His identity.[156] The angel did not give this name as a coincidence.

Forty days after Jesus's birth, Mary and Joseph took their Boy to Jerusalem along with a substitutionary offering.[157] Here, we see a strong hint that Joseph and Mary did not have a lot of money. Moses instructed parents to offer a lamb and a dove as a sacrifice for a newborn son. If they could not afford a lamb, they were to offer two doves.[158]

Joseph gave the poor man's offering. Perhaps he and Mary faced a financial bind being away from home as they were. If they were this poor, he probably couldn't even afford a donkey for her to ride on, contrary to many pictures and movies made of their trip to Bethlehem.

When Joseph and Mary traveled to the Temple, they went to perform a Jewish ritual of purification. It was a formal presentation of their firstborn Child to God. The young couple was not trying to get out of doing the things required by their faith. In fact, the Lord knew they were coming, as we will see proof of next.

---

[156] David Norris, *I AM*, (Hazelwood, MO: WAP Academic, 2009), 75-80.
[157] See Luke 2:22.
[158] See Luke 2:23-24 and Leviticus 12:6-8.

DON'T DIE YET!

IS JESUS THE FULFILLMENT of your hopes and dreams in life? Or is He on a list buried under many other things you want? Nothing should drive us like the desire to see Jesus.

Once again we find ourselves at the Temple with an elderly man. Simeon appears to be up in years. He only has one thing left on his bucket list: to see Jesus. Perhaps this was all that had ever been on his list.

The Lord promised Simeon that he would not die before seeing the Messiah.[159] Because of his prayerfulness and pure living, the Spirit of God dwelled upon Simeon. After retirement, Simeon could have said, "I've lived a good life and it is almost over. I should cut back from all this travel to the Temple." Instead, even in his sunset years, he trained his eyes to see Jesus.

What a coincidence that he would show up at the Temple at the same time as Jesus. Or was it a coincidence? You know the answer to that already. For those of us looking for Jesus, there are no mere coincidences. Simeon walked in the Spirit right up to Joseph and Mary.[160]

---

[159] See Luke 2:25-26.
[160] See Luke 2:27.

Wrinkled hands lifted up the wide-eyed Baby. Finally, Simeon got to see Jesus.[161] This man waited his entire life to see the Lord. Today many go their whole lives without Jesus, not because He has not come but because they do not want to look beyond themselves. Upon seeing Jesus, Simeon rejoiced and praised the Lord.

"I see salvation!"[162] he exclaimed. The Spirit settles on Simeon. The elderly man celebrates this Salvation (Jesus) which is for "all the peoples; a Light for revelation to the nations, and the Glory of Your people Israel."[163] Not only had the angel announced this, but now a devout Jew declares that Jesus has come for non-Jews, too! Though no Jewish believer could have imagined it at the time, Israel will have a greater impact throughout the earth by including Gentiles rather than rejecting them.

As trends go, many times the young look down on the elderly. Young people will one day be the old ones whose music, styles, and mobility will be outdated. Mary and Joseph were the types of youths to stop, listen to, and respect the voices of mature and faithful believers.

Some of my children had a great opportunity when they participated in a choir for a drama celebrating the life of missionary Nona Freeman. They got to share her emotions and struggles to put Jesus first. They also got to meet this godly woman in person and let her pray over them. She was not just another elderly lady to them but someone to respect and admire. The seniors who see Jesus need to be influencing the young ones who don't understand how great He is.

---

[161] See Luke 2:28.
[162] See Luke 2:30.
[163] Luke 2:31-32, LITV.

Simeon, walking close to the Lord, says breathtaking things to the newlyweds. Joseph seems stunned.[164] We haven't heard much about Joe or from him since the birth. Maybe he was only beginning to realize what was happening. Some people glamorize the idea of seeing angels, but it appears this old man says more to get Joseph's attention than the angel had. Perhaps for the first time, Joe sees Jesus—really sees Him.

I relate to this. I grew up in church or have always been around religious people. Too easily, our view of Jesus becomes eclipsed by the crowd and He does not stay a focus of wonder over time. Instead of being Light and Glory, He becomes a Sunday, church thing.

You don't remember the first day you noticed your mom or realized who your dad was if you grew up with them in the home. Whoever raised you from infancy feels like they have always been there. It might be a near-death experience or some other dramatic event that gets your attention to show you how important such a loved-one is.

If you have been around Jesus so much that you took Him for granted, stop and look at Him closely. I picture Joseph looking down at the Baby in his arms and weeping as the Child looked back. Jesus has to be more than the childhood church class theme or the subject of songs you learned. You don't need a near-death experience to see Him.

I've had those "look at what I have ahold of" moments just while reading the Scriptures, praying, or listening to Spirit-powered preaching. I have had those shock-and-awe moments while driving on the interstate, kneeling in prayer at my couch, or walking across a field (not necessarily in that order). Like Simeon and Joseph, I want the wonder. I want to be overwhelmed with amazement at who this Man is.

---

[164] See Luke 2:33.

The man's words amazed Mary, too. Simeon turned to her and took her surprise to another level by outlining the future of her Child.[165] Jesus will be the cause of many falling—those who reject Him will go down. And He will cause the rising of many—those who turn to Him will experience spiritual life, rising from dead works to serve the Living God.

Jesus will not only work signs but will be one. A sign points to something. This Baby points us to see God. Jesus is not a filter or a layer mask but the only correct lens through which we can see the invisible God. Because God is invisible, we will not "see" or understand Him apart from Jesus.

Many signs can mislead us from this One-Way road. The true road reveals to men and women the substance of their hearts. Jesus would soon expose prideful and self-seeking religious scams—including ones at the Temple.

Simeon tells Mary that a large sword will come down on her.[166] Sorrow would slice Mary's soul open as she watches her Son's body cut with a soldier's blade. Here we have the summary of this Baby's future life: revealing Truth, pointing the right way, and dying for many who will rise with Him.

How did Simeon see all that ahead of time? He began looking to see Jesus. Then, he saw with something more than his physical eyes.

Next Anna walks up. The Bible record did not include a prophet for centuries to this point. Here comes one at last! She shared her insights to the parents of the ultimate Prophet. She was over eighty-four years old.[167] This woman was from one of

---

[165] See Luke 2:34.
[166] See Luke 2:35, using the word for a long sword (*rhomphaia*) not just a dagger.
[167] Either she was 84 years old or had been a widow for 84 years.

the "lost tribes of Israel," those with no assigned territory. She had found her place.

If you ever wanted to find Anna, you could always locate her at the Temple where she spent her days praying and fasting. Seeing Jesus became the crowning moment of her life.[168] Neither Simeon nor Anna lived for a quiet retirement in a tropical paradise with palm trees and piña coladas. They lived to know the Lord better. What is your end game?

Before Anna saw Jesus, she first gave herself to years of prayer and fasting.[169] Believers today share her devotion and disciplines. They want to see Jesus show up in their world. Too many miss Him because they are not committed to watching for Him.

Willie Johnson was an Anna in the 20th century. She said praying and fasting should go together. She would pray and fast to the point she endangered her health.[170] Yet God spoke through her powerfully to those in need. One time, the Lord told her a young couple had lost a child and to go speak to them. From her own experience and hurts that she survived, she was able to bring healing and encouragement to that mother who had become bitter over losing her daughter to cancer.[171]

After growing up in a home focused on Jesus, I struggled in young adulthood. By age 18, I had moved out on my own and then realized my home could be whatever I wanted. If Jesus was going to be the center of my life, it was all up to me now. My dad was not there to keep daily prayer, my mom was not there reading her Bible at the kitchen table, no vehicle was leaving for church unless I was driving it. My gears slipped for a bit before they caught hold.

———————————————

[168] See Proverbs 16:31; I Timothy 5:5.
[169] Fasting would be the disciple of going without food and only drinking water for a day or days.
[170] Lori Wagner, *Through the Waters*, (Affirming Faith, 2019), 107.
[171] Ibid., 184.

Mary and Joseph could have missed their moment with these precious prayer warriors at the Temple. Sure, they "had to" go to the Temple for the sacrifices, dedication, and purification, but... they were far from home. Who in Nazareth would know if they had gone or not?

This young couple had to pay for diapers, a new stroller, baby sign language classes, or whatever babies required then. Joe's wallet still stung from the expense of the doves they roasted on the fire unto the Lord. Perhaps the thought tempted them of skipping all of this, this... religious ritual.

God knew. He knew they would be there. He expected them to do this, boring or not. He told Simeon ahead of time that they would be there. Their paths only crossed with Simeon's and Anna's because they chose to be faithful.

God knew that Joseph and Mary would do the right thing. He was so sure, He spoke for them before they did it. How do you become a faithful elderly person who prays and lives for nothing but seeing Jesus? By becoming such a person right now.

OUTSIDERS ARE WELCOME

FOR THOSE WHO HAVE NOT yet seen Jesus, He will send signs that point to Him. One person might see Jesus after surviving a car wreck. Some must go through a health crisis, the loss of job and home, or a church split before they see Jesus. Someone who has seen Jesus does not have to look in all the wrong places as they once did.

When He was born, His sign got the attention of travelers from the east.[172] One unique diamond stood out from the rest in the black-as-velvet night sky. Seeing it rise over Israel, the travelers began a long journey to see what this new and unique light in the dark was telling them.

Magi, or wise men, had educated themselves. They might have been astrologers from the area of Babylon or Persia. They may have been literal magicians or fortune-tellers. Perhaps they ruled as kings or leaders of some sort. The ancient prophet Daniel had lived in Persia (modern Iran) and introduced that country to the true God hundreds of years before this.

---

[172] See Matthew 2:1-2. In the Greek, the word for "east" is actually the word "rising" (*anatole*) and is so used because the sun rises in the east. Did they mean they saw the star rising or that they saw the star while back home in the east? Both could be true.

Being head of the Magi and one of the highest-ranking administrators, Daniel influenced them in the ways of the one true God.[173] Around five hundred years before Jesus came, this prophet taught the scholars in the East to look for the Messiah. Many generations removed from Daniel, these travelers might have studied the Scriptures and understood a secret about the great Ruler. A prophecy about a Star—a powerful leader, conquering enemies—indicated that He would rise in Judah (Judea) in the land of Israel.[174]

Even before the Magi saw Jesus, they were being led by the Spirit. Watching for significant meaning in the skies may have been what they did, but most people do not follow where God leads. They took the little that they did know of God and Scriptures and acted upon that. You must have the courage to be among the few who follow the little glimpses you have of the Lord into more and more fullness.

No voice from above told the Magi how to finish their journey to see Jesus. They needed help from humans to do that. For some reason, the Lord has made other humans part of your path to seeing Jesus. We are not meant to know Jesus alone.

Herod got into a frenzy when he heard that travelers had come to worship a new king.[175] Herod was not a Jew but an Edomite. His ancestor was Esau, the rival of his twin, Jacob, also called Israel. If an Israelite was born to be king, Herod's life was in danger. Everyone in Jerusalem was in turmoil too about what Herod would do if he went psycho, again.

Herod called in the Scripture experts.[176] I wouldn't recommend that you depend on religious professionals as your preferred way to see Jesus. Many people cannot see Jesus because the "experts" have limited them. However, even those

---

[173] See Daniel 2:13, 48-49; 5:11, 29; 6:2.
[174] See Numbers 24:17.
[175] See Matthew 2:3.
[176] See Matthew 2:4.

who have made a god of their religious tradition might find some truths when they look in Scripture.

Though not led by the Spirit, these scholars knew enough to interpret the parchment scrolls correctly on this matter. They observed the prophecy of Micah and connected it to the rising Star/Ruler in Judah. They also examined a passage about David becoming king and applied it to the coming King that would shepherd the people of Israel.[177] From all this, they determined the King would be born in Bethlehem.

Do not miss the contrast here. Bible experts in Jerusalem are discussing the coming of a Messiah that had already come. He had been born, visited Jerusalem, and already left, and they missed Him. Like most religious professionals, they were seeing their Bibles but not Jesus. In spite of their great exegesis, they had no moment of "I see Jesus." Too many churches and Christian movements today resemble this.

Just because someone does not see Jesus yet, does not mean they have no understanding. What those religion pros lacked was desire. The Magi desired to see.

Some say these travelers could have come from the Parthian empire, which might have had kings from Hebrew ancestry. Perhaps they were royalty, as some hints indicate in the prophecies. If so, their entourage would have flooded the land with camels and personnel accompanying them.[178] The main point is they did not belong there, yet they wanted to see the King.

The Lord does not prioritize those with a pedigree in religion. He shows Himself to those who seek Him. These outsiders show us that the Jews would not monopolize the

---

[177] See Matthew 2:5-6 with Micah 5:2 and II Samuel 5:2.
[178] See Isaiah 60:1-6.

Messiah.[179] All nations will benefit from this Man who walked among us.

Herod did not show his true colors to these travelers for a few reasons. If they were from Parthia, Herod will remember a time only a couple of decades before when they ruled his land. Some records indicate that rulers in Parthia were of Hebrew descent. If so, no wonder they had come to worship the new King of the Jews. Offending such a powerful force would not have been wise.

To carry as much gold and riches as they did, they needed at least a small army of bodyguards. This adds to the drama and tension causing Herod to cooperate against his will. This could also explain why "he was troubled and all Jerusalem with him."[180]

Herod tries to take advantage of these worshippers. He intends to kill the object of their worship, but cannot let them know his plan.[181] He wants to control the system. The more you see of Jesus, you will see that He gives freely, rather than manipulating for personal leverage in someone's life. If someone only sees Jesus as a threat, they are of the spirit of Herod.

You are a star. Yes, as you grow in the Lord, others will see you "rising" in Him. They will follow the light they see in you. You can lead them to see Jesus for themselves, or you can be like Herod.

If we attempt to absorb attention for ourselves, we dethrone the King in our hearts. For example, an on-looker's words like "Wow, I can tell you are close to God" can go to a person's head. We can prevent that by giving God the credit for all things and by steering people to see Jesus. We must always

---

[179] See Psalm 72:10-11, 15.
[180] Matthew 2:4, LITV.
[181] See Matthew 2:7-8.

desire to see more of Jesus also, even if an outsider or an elderly person has to be the one to point out the obvious to you.

Many religions today exploit those who are looking for Jesus. They give them false heroes in the form of superstar preachers and vocal artists. You might see more of a Christian celebrity's name than anything you hear about Jesus. They turn devotion toward God into slavish infatuation with a church building or denomination. Yes, the spirit of Herod still survives. Don't let it live in you.

Herod never saw the star. We can't allow ourselves to become like him—so dense we cannot see the things leading us to see Jesus. Let's not be so distant we have to depend on what others see of Jesus and fail to see for ourselves.

Don't stay around people who cannot and will not see Him. After "having heard the king, they departed. And, behold! The star" appeared before them again![182] Sometimes you will see Jesus when you get away from people who are spiritual black holes.

The travelers were beside themselves with joy when they saw the star reappear.[183] They had not seen Jesus yet but freaked out at just the signs leading to Him. I have never seen a man on a camel do a happy dance, but I doubt they cared who was watching.

Joy is good, but I have watched many people stop there. The Lord takes away their shame and they experience joy as they get close to Him. To them, this is much better than what they have ever known and they feel complete. They stop short of following through to knowing Jesus and settle for the thrill of

---

[182] Matthew 2:9, LITV.
[183] See Matthew 2:10.

getting close. Those seekers from the East would not stop until they made it all the way to Jesus.

What about you? Are you still looking at the sensational? Are you so close to Jesus that you have joy but not Him? Is Jesus still a religious thing to you? Or is He a friend?

The religious experts in Jerusalem knew the facts about Him, but never touched Him. Don't discourage those who are rejoicing over the star. Help them get to Jesus!

Before the Magi saw Jesus, they had to leave their comfort zone (and so must we). Only then, did they get to Jesus. If we take it literally, the term for "worshipping" means they fell down and kissed the ground.[184] Something about seeing Jesus changes your values. Instead of hanging onto their treasures, the magi reached into their saddlebags and gave Jesus gifts fit for a king. The closer you get to Jesus, the more you will find yourself giving up the things you used to cling to.

The gold sparkled at His feet. The woody scent of frankincense filled the room. From the container of myrrh wafted a pungent medicinal smell, an aroma of wealth. Their gift-giving teaches us to bring our best to Jesus.

They did not bring socks, diapers, and rattles to this baby shower. They didn't stop at the dollar store and grab what they could along the way. If your giving to Jesus has just been a few hours on the weekend or stray minutes through your day—why don't you become as devout as these guys? They did not know what religious tradition expected of them or they would have done much less. They did not bring minimums; they gave because hope was born.

---

[184] See Matthew 2:11. The Greek word for worship (*proskuneo*) carries the idea of kissing the hand or falling face down to the ground.

If your giving matched your amazement at how great Jesus is, what would it look like? How would your financial priorities change? How would your schedule change?

TAKE ANOTHER PATH

GOD SPOKE TO DANIEL, the ancient prophet, in dreams and visions. The travelers from the East were tuned to hear from God that way, too. At times, the Lord still speaks to young and old, men and women, through dreams and visions.[185] After the Magi saw Jesus, they learned in a dream to avoid Herod and go home another way.[186]

These gift-giving travelers give us another lesson. Not only had they seen Jesus, but they heard from heaven, too. We would not be having this conversation about seeing spiritual things if someone had not been hearing that inaudible voice.

Zachariah had struggled to accept the Lord's voice. Mary heard and accepted immediately. Joseph heard from heaven and immediately changed his actions.

Herod and the priests in Jerusalem were not hearing from heaven. They had the written Word but had grown deaf to the Word in their hearts and blind to the Word in the manger. These outsiders heard and saw. When the Lord spoke to them in a dream, they obeyed Him rather than the words of the most powerful man in Israel.

---

[185] Acts 2:16-17.
[186] See Matthew 2:12.

Too often people glimpse Jesus and then go right back to Herod. Even though the religious professionals helped them understand where to look for Jesus, the dream warned them not to go back to that system. Jerusalem was not hearing the voice of the Lord. They closely guarded His commands on their dusty scrolls, but He was not dwelling in their hearts.

We do not look for flaws in the religious efforts of others, but we must be careful who we follow. Sometimes our loyalties can develop toward the system, scholars, or individuals who helped us get closer to Jesus. If that system is not Spirit-powered, though, we must move on.

The religious experts got the Magi to Jesus, but the travelers had to make the hard choice to turn away from Jerusalem. Scripture warns us about religious groups that have an appearance of godliness but lack Spirit power. If we are among them, we must desert their ranks.[187] Man-made religion might have been where you got your start on the journey of faith, but ultimately you want to follow Jesus.

Joseph dreamed again. Another white-robed angel spoke, "Rise up!"[188] From his actions, we see Joe is a wise man, too. As any true believer should, he hears from the Lord (though this will not happen only in dreams).

He and Mary follow the angel's instructions to journey south and east to Egypt. This journey of at least 100 miles had to be a rough trip on the young mother. It is likely that they used some of the gold and treasures the easterners had given Jesus to finance the journey. Perhaps they stopped at their local Rent-a-Donkey. Maybe they splurged and got an UberBurro.

---

[187] See II Timothy 3:5.
[188] Matthew 2:13, LITV.

Joseph took his family to Egypt as the Patriarch Joseph did almost two millennia prior.[189] Mary, named after Moses's sister Miriam,[190] would be living in the land of the Nile as they had. She, too, would be watching over a special child saved from a wicked king.

Departing at night like ancient Israel fleeing Egypt, Joseph led his family to a place that was safe for the time.[191] There, in unfamiliar territory, Joseph and Mary found themselves once again in God's perfect will. As awkward as that trip was, they were fulfilling prophecy... again.

Yes, Jesus and His family were refugees for a time. God has always taught His people to be loving and supportive of foreigners in town. As many as 70-80% of international students in the USA never enter an American home or a church. What if you could be the difference in helping some of them see Jesus? What if they, like the Magi, returned home with news of the great King and led their families to see Jesus?

Herod realized that the Magi had made a fool of him. Proud people hate when others mock them. Since all he could see was himself, he tried to prevent anyone else from seeing Jesus. If pride drives our motives, we will miss seeing Jesus, too.

Herod calculated the age of Jesus based on what the travelers had told him about when the star first appeared. Then, he ordered the death of every child under two years.[192] Though he put on a religious front, Herod wanted to kill the Truth. We can't trust all people who act spiritual—not even the ones who build fancy religious buildings.

---

[189] See the history of Jacob's son named Joseph in Genesis chapters 37-47.
[190] See the history of Miriam in Exodus 2:1-10.
[191] See Matthew 2:14 and Exodus 12:31.
[192] See Matthew 2:16.

In a striking similarity, an ancient Pharaoh tried to kill all the Hebrew boys in the days of Moses.[193] Like Moses, Jesus narrowly escapes. Jesus is the New Moses,[194] bringing in a new covenant, a theme we will see again.

When the prophet said, "I called My son out of Egypt,"[195] the Lord was speaking about Israel. Matthew uses that passage as a lens to show us Jesus as the replacement for Israel as well![196] By preserving the nation of Israel, God preserved the offspring of Abraham through whom would come The Offspring—Jesus the Messiah. So, twice, God preserved His Son via Egypt.

Jesus is now a young Child, not an infant. Given the forty days it took until His presentation in Jerusalem, and the length of the journey for the magi to arrive, much time had gone by since the night of the singing angels and shouting shepherds. Jesus was probably over a year old at this point.

The murder of unsuspecting children troubles me deeply. Though Bethlehem numbered among the smaller towns, there may have been as many as two dozen deaths. This massacre did not even make the news under Herod the Great's brutal rule. Many other atrocities stack up against him. All who stood for righteousness found that man loathsome.

It saddens me further to think that these innocent deaths could have been prevented. The Scriptures warned what would

---

[193] See Exodus 2.
[194] A popular story among Jews around the time of Christ said a magician had warned Pharaoh (king of Egypt) that a new ruler would be born among the Hebrews. This, according to the tale, is what triggered Pharaoh to order the murder of Hebrew boys. Most Jews would have been familiar with this legend and could have seen the direct correlation between it and the story of Jesus. See R. T. France, *Matthew: An Introduction and Commentary*, Vol. I, Leon Morris, Ed. (Downers Grove, IL: Intervarsity, 1985).
[195] Hosea 11:1, LITV.
[196] See Matthew 2:15.

happen.[197] Joseph was listening to heaven and escaped. The people in the religious headquarters knew the prophecies but did not warn anyone. The parents in Bethlehem should have read the Scriptures for themselves and prepared their own families.

Similar atrocities are happening today. That same spirit of Herod is still killing babies. Not only political leaders but also some religious ones are allowing or promoting harm to innocent ones. How will you make a difference? Will you "rescue Jesus" from the destroyer today by helping a defenseless child?

---

[197] See Matthew 2:17-18 with Jeremiah 31:15.

WHEN GOD CAMPED OUT

O NE YEAR, after many long days of writing, I developed some eye pain from the glare off my old CRT computer screen. To this day if I stare at a laptop, phone, or another screen up close, my eyes will begin to ache. After years of avoiding prolonged screen time, I decided I had to change something since I am a writer and must look at a screen.

The remedy to my problem came with a pair of blue-block glasses. This is a rather non-trendy-looking set of spectacles with amber lenses that filter out the harmful light waves on the blue end of the spectrum. These save my eyes and I can work even in a dark room now with no eye fatigue. The yellow "window panes" in these specs change the look of everything, though. What helped my eyes in one area now tinges my perspective on everything else I see, while I wear those glasses.

To understand some of the angles the Gospels take to present Jesus, we have to understand the "glasses" people of that day were looking through. Some of their darkly tinted lenses caused them to miss Jesus. Primarily, the people of Israel saw everything through the "Moses" filter.

Moses led the people through the wilderness and up to the Promised Land. He made his claim to fame when he organized the building of the Lord's "house." It was a gigantic tent out in the wilderness called the Tabernacle.

This portable building consisted of two rooms, the front one larger than the back. Three pieces of golden furniture filled the front room. In the smaller room, a golden box served as a portable throne. It was as if God sat there to rule on earth, though He is invisible. Though their Yahweh[198] God could not be seen, He appeared to the Israelites as a crackling flame in the night sky and as a cloud pillar over that tent in daylight.

Hundreds of years later, King Solomon built a permanent building. God "moved out" of His Tabernacle into that stone construction called the Temple. Their God was in a box, so to speak. Through that filter, Jesus's contemporaries stared at Him.

Of course, God is bigger than any building humans can build. We cannot contain Him. We cannot build Him a proper throne.

The Gospel of John throws down this snapshot, saying, "the Word became flesh and tabernacled among us"[199] and shattered the filter so many were viewing God through. Jews knew immediately what John meant when he said this. The word often translated as "dwelled"[200] also means to set up a tent. They used this word in reference to the Tabernacle of Moses.

---

[198] The pronunciation of the name for God in the Old Testament is a bit of an enigma. Due to many years of the Name not being pronounced and the many years Hebrew ceased to be a spoken language, the correct pronunciation of this name has been lost (as has "correct" pronunciation of any Hebrew word). Therefore, we have elected to use the word "Yahweh" in this book as a representation for YHWH or YHVH or JHVH, which are the English attempts at capturing the essence of that original word. Just know there is a lot of discussion on how to handle this word properly in any language and we don't pretend to have it all figured out.

[199] John 1:14, LITV.

[200] Greek *skeñoo*. This word also applies to the Tabernacle in the old covenant.

God found a suitable dwelling place in the humanity of Jesus, not a fancy tent in the wilderness or an ornate building downtown. (Besides, downtown was getting crowded.) God did not take this dwelling place for a short-term stay—this was God's new abode.[201]

Remember, the Creator made flesh; now He has been made flesh. Why? So that flesh (humanity) can become what He is—eternal. The Creator is done camping out. With a permanent connection to humanity, He is here to stay.

John was not done smashing their distorted old lenses. He continued saying that they could see His "glory" in a new and amazing way.[202] Though we do not use the word "glory" in typical conversations, the term in the original language referred to something brilliantly bright or something on a level above everything around it. To see Jesus is not to see another guy. He radiates with power and wisdom above anyone else who has ever lived.

Ever felt like God was out of reach? If so, you are not alone. In the past, other devout people tried to zoom in on a distant God who was out of their reach, but Jesus brings God so close it's almost easy to miss Him. The humanity of Jesus that they saw was much different than the common person. Yet those who noticed Him saw the splendor of who Jesus is.

Moses asked to see God's glory, but the Lord only showed him a part—the lesser side of Himself.[203] The people spoke of the presence of God over Moses's Tabernacle as His Glory Cloud. The fullness of that Glory appeared in the Word-Made-Flesh.[204] We have His favor on top of favor.

_____

[201] Norris, *I AM*, 72.
[202] John 1:14.
[203] See Exodus 33:19-23.
[204] John 1:16, LITV.

Even the best glasses, such as Moses, have to be removed to see Jesus. Scripture explains that many who follow this great man have a blinder over their spiritual eyes. The veil of the law of Moses must be removed for us to see Jesus clearly.[205]

Jews thought nothing was higher than the writings of Moses, called *Torah,* or the "Law." Jesus brought something greater than the stone tablets carried by that great leader in Hebrew history: "For the Law was given through Moses, but grace and truth came through Jesus Christ."[206] Torah's demanding code condemned those who did not behave. Jesus brought the power to live right.

Did Moses know how much more God had planned for people of faith? There was so much he did not get to see. No matter how much my eyes have opened to see the Lord, I am still light-years behind. I must never grow arrogant or comfortable in my knowledge of Him and how He works.

The Tabernacle had a blueprint with exact dimensions and required materials: leather, blue/purple cloth, white linen, wood posts, gold, brass, and more. The blueprint of God's own identity existed from the dawn of time. Only the physically sired child of God would meet the specifications to display the invisible God. Meet Jesus, God's new Tabernacle.

Those who see Jesus correctly today become part of that blueprint. We become whole new people, who were "born not of blood, nor of the will of the flesh, nor of the will of man, but were born of God."[207] We will learn much more about this complete transformation beyond the typical religious phrase "get saved."

In the next book in this series, we will take some time to see what it means to become a new person in Jesus. Those who join God's DNA also reflect His identity, becoming a house where

---

[205] See II Corinthians 3:13-18.
[206] John 1:17, LITV.
[207] See John 1:12-13.

He dwells by His Spirit, too. We are all needed—no window left out, every cabinet in place. You and I are the filters through which others will see God.

While on a video call once with my children and my wife, I accidentally selected a mask that made my lips turn black and had spiders dropping into the scene. My kids screamed and my wife put the phone face down. They did not want to see me like that.

What if you have been looking at Jesus with a mask of some sort? What if some bad impression someone gave you of Him left you looking through a mutated image? Might some false belief system have put a mask on your Jesus and you have been looking at Him all wrong?

The Gospels bring in some pretty edgy pics. John has to point out the wrong filters. He aims, focuses, and shoots down misconceptions about Jesus Christ.

I know I have had misperceptions about Him. I'm sure I still do. I keep going back to the original, finding and removing those edited layers. I want Jesus unfiltered. I want Him original and not defined by manmade perspectives.

The record of Jesus begins with the out-of-this-world encounter of God becoming flesh. The Christmas season has put an awful filter over Jesus, often making Him seem like child's play. The Christmas Jesus is cuddly and soft and so pastel. The real Jesus is much more than a Precious Moments figure.

Without trimmings or trinkets, Scripture shows how cataclysmic this moment was. While we must see the finer details of manger and myrrh, we must also see the explosiveness of the moment. The Inventor of time, physics, and matter joined Himself to these limitations. Now, we can join with His limitlessness.

Imagine a friend introducing you to a man, saying, "iPhones came by Steve Jobs, but there is new and better technology by Bob Smith here." Or "Facebook came by Mark Zuckerberg, but you have to see this new social app by Jane Doe." Such an introduction lets us know the new innovation must be amazing if it tops one of the most popular inventions.

Likewise, John says, "For the Law was given through Moses, but grace and truth came through Jesus Christ."[208] Since Jews held Moses in the highest esteem, to present Jesus like this was to shock them. John does not present Moses plus Jesus, but Jesus in place of Moses. Such a gospel demands decision.

Moses had something of a "face to face" relationship with God like a person would have with a close friend.[209] Yet John says, "No one has seen God at any time."[210] The Lord even pointed out to Moses, "You cannot see My face; for no man shall see Me, and live."[211] The man got close, though.

Only "the Begotten," the one "in the bosom," declares Him. If you have something valuable to carry, you often clutch it close to your chest (bosom). The Father cherishes the Son above all people.

Not only is Jesus higher than any patriarch or prophet of the past, but He is the One qualified to announce the Father in His fullness.[212] Jesus is the face of God. The invisible God has made Himself known in flesh: "For it is the God who commanded light to shine out of darkness, who has shone in our hearts to give the light of the knowledge of the glory of God in the face of Jesus Christ."[213] As we see Jesus, we are not seeing God through a filter—we are seeing God in the only correct lens.

---

[208] John 1:17, LITV.
[209] See Exodus 33:11; Deuteronomy 34:10.
[210] See John 1:18.
[211] Exodus 33:20, NKJV.
[212] See John 1:18; Matthew 11:27.
[213] II Corinthians 4:6, NKJV.

We find everything about what God is in the Man Jesus Christ. He is the image of the invisible God in whom dwells all the fullness of the Father.[214] This Man is the physical completion of almighty God. This is why the prophet could say that the Son would be "Mighty God" and "Eternal Father."[215]

If the Jewish people had to have their eyes opened from tradition and misplaced loyalties, what about Christians today? Do you have a Catholic, Lutheran, Methodist, Baptist, Mormon, Pentecostal, or non-denominational filter applied to Jesus? Some are seeing Him through an overlay of Martin Luther, John Calvin, Charles Parham, Billy Graham, John MacArthur, Joyce Meyers, T. D. Jakes, or Joel Osteen. Imagine seeing Jesus without all the backdrops and layers of modern Christianity. I can think of a few Moses-like glasses (persons) John would call out if he were writing today.

Could you or I have become attached to certain people, traditions, denominations, and beliefs that are not purely from Jesus Christ? Could we be seeing Him through rose-colored glasses rather than reality? Just as those deeply religious people were in for the shock of their lives, so we should be ready for wake-up moments in order to see the Man from Bethlehem.

What the five books of Moses are to the Old Covenant, the four Gospels and Acts are to the New. As we move forward in this series of seeing Jesus, we will not rush over these writings. We are going to take our time to grasp everything Jesus taught.[216] Not only do we not want to miss anything Jesus did or said, but we also want to pass these things on to others.

As you help others come and see Jesus, you also will see Him in an all-new way. The process of helping others see Him challenged what I thought I already knew. I had to find answers.

---

[214] See Colossians 1:15, 19.
[215] See Isaiah 9:6.
[216] See Matthew 28:19-20.

What I found changed me. Through this and the coming books, the Jesus of Scripture will change you, too.

UNEXPECTED PERFECTION

HEROD THE GREAT DIED. Some funerals should be celebrations—dressed in neon, not black—playing jazz, not blues. The people of Israel wanted to send balloons instead of flowers.

Messages traveled slowly in those days. An angel broke the evening news to Joseph.[217] Assuming the threat of danger for his family had passed, Joseph headed home as soon as he got the word.[218]

I imagine Mary had plans for the house when they got back: some new drapes and a total makeover of the main room. She was looking forward to seeing new friends and Joseph's family when they arrived. Some of them hadn't seen Jesus walking yet.

Suddenly, another annoyance changed their course. Archelaus, Herod the Great's son, had taken charge.[219] He was as bad as the wicked king he replaced. Discovering this news and hearing from heaven in another dream, Joseph had to not only change course but had to make another big life adjustment:

---

[217] See Matthew 2:19-20.
[218] See Matthew 2:21.
[219] See Matthew 2:22.

moving the family back to Galilee. That's about like moving from Long Island to the Bronx or from Virginia Beach to Chicago.

Apparently, Joseph and Mary had set up house in Bethlehem and intended to stay. They only left because of the danger. Now, because of Herod's hateful son, he would have to find another place to work and live. Mary wondered how and where she was going to set up house this time.

Galilee included more Gentiles. Was that any place to raise a child? Would it be better or worse now than when she grew up there? Nazareth was near that Roman city Antipas was rebuilding stone by stone. Would it be safe with him coming nearby? So much to consider, so many unknowns.

Through all the turmoil, we see God's hand still at work. Mary and Joseph moved to Nazareth and Jesus fulfilled another prophecy: being called a Nazarene. One of those early classified leaks said that the Messiah would be the "Branch" (*natzer*) from David's family line.[220]

Not only did the family settle in the town of Nazareth, but it is possible Joseph got work as a stonemason in the nearby city of Sepphoris. There, Herod Antipater, half-brother to the meanie in Judea, was building a theater that would seat 4,000 people![221] The city had burned about the time Jesus's family was in Egypt. There would be enough work there for Joseph and for Jesus when he got older. Antipas, the common nickname for Antipater, was hiring many builders ("carpenters") to construct his dream.

So many things leave us feeling like life is so random. It is and it isn't. Multiple times "random" events yanked this young couple from one place to the next. Mary knew a sword would

---

[220] See Matthew 2:23. This popular messianic title came from the branch (*netzer*) in Isaiah 11:1 (4:2). See also Jeremiah 23:5; 31:6; 33:15; Zechariah 3:8; 6:12. This title could also come from the name for the watchmen (*nâtsar*) in Jeremiah 31:6. *Nazir* also means one holy to God. See Keener, *Matthew*, 114.

[221] https://en.wikipedia.org/wiki/Sepphoris

pierce her soul. Already she was feeling the raw edge of that blade. Think back to what she has been through:

Joseph: "Mary, we have to go to Bethlehem."

Mary: "Do they need you there right now? Why not after the baby is born? Shouldn't the government give exemptions for pregnant women? I'm coming, I'm coming."

Also Mary: "Wait... what? The Scriptures say the Promised One would be born in Bethlehem. Whoa... do you think...?"

Joseph: "Mary, we have to go to Jerusalem."

Mary: "I have to walk that far when I am only six weeks post-partum? I'd like to see some man lose a ten-pound tumor and walk halfway across the country. Why do the women who have girls get to wait almost twelve weeks before going to offer sacrifice? I'll get my stuff."

Also Mary: "Whoa—now here's a fellow who says God told him we were going to be here. Oh, look, a grandma, too! God knew we would do this?!"

Joseph: "Mary, we have to get back to Bethlehem."

Mary: "You know, we could move back to Nazareth now. I am sure you could find work up there just as easy as down here. I mean, at least I would be near my mother and she could teach me stuff. A girl needs her mom when she's had a baby, you know? Never mind, let's head back."

Also Mary: "Wait, did those guys say a star in the night sky told them we were here? If we had moved away they would have found an empty house! And those gifts are lit!"

Joseph: "Mary, we have to leave for Egypt tonight!"

Mary: "You've got to be kidding! Why didn't you tell me you would be this kind of husband? In the dead of night? How will I pack? Where are we going this time?"

Also Mary: "Hold the donkey! I just heard that Herod sacked the town after we left! That was a narrow miss!"

Joseph: "Mary, we can go back to Israel."

Mary: "This time, I'm ready to go. I didn't even get to say goodbye to your mom. You know, she has been very helpful and I wouldn't mind so much if—what? Not going to Bethlehem?! You know this is too much. A girl needs to know how to plan. I am not an old robe to be tossed about—I have feelings and hopes and dreams."

Also Mary: "Wait a minute. Don't tell me. We are in God's perfect will again! Jesus will be called a Nazarene. I should have known. How does He do that?"

What if each one of us allowed ourselves to see God in the random craziness of life? In the next few chapters, we are going to explore how to get headed in the right direction in spite of the surprises.

You, Revisited

L ET'S GO BACK to your childhood. Did you cringe when I said that? Sorry.

Everyone has good memories from childhood and some not-so-nice incidents. I don't know which way the scale tips for you. But many adults today still struggle with seeds planted in their childhood.

It is dangerous to be a kid in many ways. Some children didn't know their parents. Some kids lost a mom or dad to some heroic cause like rescuing people from a fire. Some lost their parents who were nothing like heroes at all. Some children were adopted by loving parents. Some weren't. Some grew older without growing up. Some only remember being shunted around in the foster system. Some children split in two with their parents' divorce. Some grew up in poverty, leaving them fearful of the future and jaded against having children of their own. Some saw such horrors of abuse that they blocked them from their memory.

We don't have any stories from Jesus's childhood other than the trip to Egypt and moving back to Nazareth. What we do have is a summary of His progression: He grew and became strong in spirit. Jesus grew in wisdom.[222] Just as He started out with a small body that grew into a mature body, so He grew mentally, emotionally, and relationally.

Mentally, He memorized Scripture. Emotionally, He grew to understand those typical human feelings. Relationally, He grew to understand other people's emotions and how to read them quickly.

Often we make it to adulthood with a few childish ways still lingering that we need to mature out of. A child matures by having a strong spirit. Jesus did not have a stubborn spirit. He was a young Man with resolve, walking in purpose and identity.

Another way of saying, "strong in spirit" is "emotionally mature." Are you mature enough that your emotions do not rule you? Too many adults today feel they have to do whatever their feelings dictate. Slam the door. Buy the overpriced item. Watch the video. We should have gotten over impulse-driven living by adulthood. Jesus overcame that as a Child.

Your spirit should be stronger than your feelings. A mature person rules his or her spirit.[223] Those who do not rule their spirits will be invaded and destroyed like a house with no walls. Emotionally stable people do not need someone to pull them back up when they get to moping or pitying themselves. Stable people do not vent on others just because it feels good to let off scream.

As I have grown in the Lord and led others to see Jesus, I have learned the importance of this part of development. After many years of being a faithful-to-church Christian, I still had issues. I lived in ruts of impatience with my children, yelling about this, demanding about that. The sad part is I did not realize my childish behavior. I still needed my wisdom to grow up to match my height. For Jesus, both kept pace.

---

[222] See Luke 2:40.
[223] See Proverbs 16:32; 25:28.

You cannot claim Jesus is the answer if your emotions are your master. Your feelings are not you. Just like you don't act on every thought, you don't have to act on every feeling. Think of an emotional storm like a rainstorm. It might be a reality you have to deal with, but you put on a coat and boots and find a way through until it passes.

Fear might try to get you down. Anger might make you want to explode. Yet you keep going because you know who you are in Jesus Christ. You are not going to let the moment, event, or irritant define you.

More than bandage or hide our emotions, we are going to learn concrete ways of overcoming our childish flaws as we see more and more of Jesus. Here are some lack-of-wisdom things we overcome: entitlement mentality, self-pity, and low self-image. Perhaps you only felt noticed as a child when you had new clothes. That could leave a person always wanting new stuff to feel worthwhile. A person might have gotten his or her way by pouting or crying like a child and still drains others' emotions to get noticed.

It is hard to say how much His parents contributed to His development. It would be intimidating to raise God-in-flesh. Regardless, Mary and Joseph did for Jesus what parents should do for their children today: connect them to others who share the faith.

Taking Jesus to Passover feasts in Jerusalem was Mary and Joseph's way of helping Him attach to the big picture of their faith rather than only their local gathering.[224] Even the youngsters need to go to conferences and large events. Too often, it is easier to leave the children with family or a sitter. Children need to be involved in seeing adults celebrate their faith and respond to preaching. If all they see is children's ministry, they

[224] See Luke 2:41-42.

do not get a bigger picture of how they should participate when older.

At this mid-point in my life, I have the advantage of a perspective including good parents who raised me and good children the Lord has given my wife and me. I am grateful for the many childhood memories I have from large events where many who loved Jesus had gathered. I have also seen the benefit of my children making connections with others beyond our local group, too.

Try as they might to raise Jesus well, his parents felt like failures at least once. Twelve-year-old Jesus was missing from the group.[225] Days went by, and they did not find Him.

"Joseph, how will we find Him?"

"He'll turn up."

"I can't believe I've lost the promised Son. All heaven showered me with favor and attention and now I've gone and done something like this. What will God say?"

"He lost Adam in the garden, didn't He?"

"Not funny. Joseph, I can't even think of where to start looking."

That is not exactly what they said, but I imagine this couple stressed out, driving their donkey all over town, trying to get the child-tracking app to open on their phones. I'm exaggerating. They probably only had one phone; times were hard then.

One time, I was out grocery shopping with the family and our youngest had fallen asleep in his car seat. My oldest daughter

_____

[225] See Luke 2:43.

told me he was sleeping as she left the car to go into the store with everyone else. I nodded and then parked the vehicle. I started flipping through social media on my phone and then got bored. I thought, "Why am I sitting out here? I should run on inside where I can be with my wife and children." So, I hopped out and hurried inside.

As I walked up to the family, a few quizzical looks greeted me. So much for thinking they would be glad to see me. "Where's the baby?" somebody asked. I paused and felt the dumbest I have felt in a long time. I ran back to the van and found him still sound asleep. Fortunately, it was neither hot nor cold outside.

Jesus's parents lost Him for longer than the 60 seconds I did my son. They were good parents, yet they left Him behind. Even good people make mistakes.

These parents had a community of faith that influenced their son as well.[226] Believers should not have to raise their children in isolation. A local church should have those who will speak into your son or daughter's life. If you do not have family members in truth, you need to let the church be your extended family. Most children today are influenced by an anti-faith community more than by their own parents.

In spite of their close community of faith, nobody knew where He was. For three days, young Miriam worried about her little Man. Well, she could hardly say little. Next year the community would recognize Him as one of the men.

Where would they have found you at age twelve? If your parents did not know you were missing for three days and you could get away with anything, where would it have been? Who would you have hung out with? What would you have done?

---

[226] See Luke 2:44-45.

For three days, Jesus has been right where they brought Him, at the Temple.[227] At twelve-years-old, Jesus is our example of what a true believer should be like. If we love God, we will be found among those who love the things of God. Our loved ones should expect to find us searching the Scriptures, praying, and talking with those who share those same values.

You don't have to be conceived from Heaven to love the things of God as a young person. Back at the time when Babylon sacked Jerusalem, four teens loved the things of God so much they were willing to risk their lives for Him by not eating the foods that were devoted to false gods.[228] The Lord rewarded them and promoted them to important leadership positions, next to the king himself.

What was happening for you around the ages of 10, 11, 12, and 13? Those pivotal years are often when we start searching. Most of us don't know what we are searching for so we look down any path for fulfillment. Perhaps you started desiring to do something to improve the world or to find excitement in life. Your longing for God began to awaken around this time, too.

Coming up to twelve years old, I was smashing milk cartons with my friends, chasing girls, or playing video games. By age thirteen, I had heard the voice of the Lord enough to know He had a purpose for my life. I began soaking in the Scriptures. Prayer and fasting became a quest in my life. I loved talking to prayerful men and women and learning from those who spent their lives studying the Holy Book.

Jesus shows us what a normal human being is like since Adam set the wrong example. If a normal twelve-year-old loves the things of God, how much more should those who are older? Devoted believers do not need someone twisting their arms to get them to read, pray, or give.

----

[227] See Luke 2:46
[228] See Daniel 1:8-15.

At the Temple, men with long white beards looked down at the smooth-faced boy. Seeing Jesus is not just a matter of reading the Bible. We see Jesus here opening their understanding to the Scriptures.[229] If we are going to see Jesus, we need Him to open the written Word to us.

Jesus illustrates two qualities of a mature believer: they can listen and ask questions. Jesus was teaching by listening. His understanding and answers amazed them. How do you get sixty-year-old experts to listen to a kid? Not by telling them what you know. Ask them questions.

Later, we will see Jesus continue this Q & A strategy as a training process. Want to help others see Jesus? Learn to ask thought-provoking questions and listen to their hearts, not just their words when they answer.

---

[229] See Luke 2:47.

DAD'S INTERESTS

ACH YEAR, Mary and Joseph would take the eighty-mile journey south to Jerusalem, raising their children with respect for holy things.[230] Then, they could not find Jesus for three days. Have you ever gone through a time that you couldn't find Jesus? Where did you look? Sometimes I waste good time looking in all the places I want Him to be, but He's predictable. Look in the Scriptures. He's always there.

Mary was like, "I was having panic attacks, Jesus. I've been worried sick! I haven't been able to sleep for three days." At least I imagine her saying something like that.

"Quit reading your Bible, Son, we have a life to attend to." It would not be likely that their home had a Bible. He had to go to the synagogue to read the Holy Scrolls, most likely. Whatever Jesus's situation, we see He had a strong desire for spiritual things. This is what twelve-year-old you should have been like.

Are you as spiritual as a seventh-grader? Looking at young Jesus is a chance for us to gauge our maturity. Jesus is the original image of what a human should be, remember. Are we as mature as a human should be? I get irritated at perpetual adolescence—adults acting like children. But if I am not as

---

[230] See Luke 2:41.

devoted and spiritually aware as this young Man, I have not matured past age twelve yet.

While helping missionaries overseas, I remember a storm threatening the island. Some teen girls from the church showed up at the Bible school and church campus. They said they were afraid of the storm but knew they would be safe if they got to God's house. These young people who had grown up in less-than-ideal homes gravitated to places and people dedicated to Jesus.

Of course, a building is not special in itself. Church campuses include buildings dedicated to the things of God and people who love Him. The Temple was such a place. Want to see Jesus? Go where the Bible is honored. Go where Jesus is giving understanding.

Then we have the first recorded words of Christ: He asks questions. This is how God works in the flesh. An influencer stirs others to think for themselves. You are a spiritual influencer in the lives of those around you to help them think through their presuppositions.

"Why did you seek Me?"[231] The young Man seems shocked that His parents would not think to look for Him in the Father's house. "Did you not know that I must be busy in the affairs of My Father?"[232] Mature enough now to realize His identity, Jesus sees that Joseph is not His biological father.

His parents "did not understand the word which He spoke to them."[233] Sometimes Jesus is more complex than we can comprehend. Not only was the tweenage Jesus mystifying, but we will also see later that even His close followers struggled to understand Him.

---

[231] Luke 2:49, NKJV.
[232] Luke 2:49, LITV.
[233] Luke 2:50, LITV.

"He went with them and came to Nazareth and was being subject to them."[234] Being a revelatory twelve-year-old doesn't mean you won't have to keep your room clean and brush your teeth. The original language here shows that He submitted to His parents in an ongoing, continual process.

Core to His nature, God submits. This feels counterintuitive because we would think the Highest Being would only give commands. Yet here, God in human experience willingly submitted. He respected His mother.

It feels like Jesus has seen more at the Temple this year than He had before. His human mind processed it all at a deeper level. He consciously saw who He was and what He was to do. Then He submitted and His ministry had to wait 18 years.

You also will go through your awakening and development at different levels. Though you have a glimpse of your identity and mission for the Lord, that does not mean it begins at that moment. Most of the time, one has to wait until the right timing to go and do those things to which he or she has been called. We will see the key to this timing as the Gospels progress.

Young Jesus understood who He was. His parents didn't. You might rejoice because you know who you are in the Lord, but that does not mean others will understand you.

Jesus continued to progress forward after that defining moment in Jerusalem. His height increased; His wisdom also grew. He found favor with others and walked in the favor of God.[235]

Jesus had favor with people. Certain ways of thinking will stir up strife between us and others; even as a child, Jesus found a point of likeability. Aside from social integration, we want to

---

[234] Luke 2:51, LITV.
[235] See Luke 2:52.

connect with the God of all creation. Jesus grew in favor with God.

We are wanting to see Jesus and learn from Him. Disfavor with God comes from going against His plans for our lives. This young Man did the things God expected of any human, in character, prayer, and love of Scripture. Dysfunctional humans are either out of favor with others, stirring up disfavor with God, or are at odds with both.

Have you ever seen a boy crying and demanding that his mom get him something at the superstore? The mother yells, "You aren't getting nothin', you cry baby!" Neither the child nor the parent in such a situation knows how to find favor with others. The child is undisciplined because his mom is. If she knew how to rule her own spirit and find favor with him, he would learn by that example how to interact with her and others.

Good parents raise their children to find favor. Regardless of your upbringing, find favor with others! A follower of Jesus builds relationships rather than neglecting or destroying them.

It is not hard to figure out if you have favor with people. Look beneath their noses. Simply put, smiles indicate when you have found favor with them; scowls show they dislike you. We do not live for approval or acceptance from everyone, but we do need to have an amicable relationship with society in general.

Being like Jesus means finding favor among your fellow humans. Even though many get offended, you do not go around offending people if you can help it. As much as possible, live in peace with everyone.[236]

People who are aware of themselves and others can find favor. This self-awareness and social intelligence come hand-in-hand with emotional stability. While we should be educated, our

[236] See Romans 12:18-19.

emotional awareness of ourselves and others will take our friendships much further than intellect alone.

As we shall see, Jesus was aware of His emotions and could speak about them. You have lived through those awkward situations where individuals were not aware of their emotional triggers. They overreact at times without notice, getting everyone else sick on their emotional rollercoaster.

Age only indicates time, not levels of wisdom. It would be nice if life were like a video game and you could say, "I just cleared level 29 and moved up to 30." That sounds impressive. However, some 50-year-olds are just 20-year-olds who have repeated the same foolish mistakes for 30 years. Some 30-year-olds have not gotten to the level of 12-year-old Jesus. Jesus had wisdom as a child. A life with purpose develops more maturity and wisdom than a life lived for the fun of it.

What is disfavor? For one example, the neighbors of the poor man hate him.[237] Of course, we should not feel this way about our underprivileged neighbors, but we need to realize that if we come across with a poor-mouth or slovenly way of living, we turn others against us. Think about others; treat them the way you want to be treated. Don't borrow their mower and break it. Don't receive from others and not reward them in some way.

A few years ago, a new family moved into the worst house in our neighborhood. My wife, our children, and I stopped by one day to be neighborly. The house had been painted blue on one side and a pukey mustard color on the other. Someone had repaired one section of the exterior wall using roofing shingles as siding. The family was just as sketchy.

When we pulled into the driveway, the woman looked embarrassed to be seen in her thong bikini. She put up the lid on

---

[237] See Proverbs 14:20; 19:7.

the grill and never came out from behind it the whole time we visited with her four little children, her husband, and his friend.

The hubby and his dude had stomped out from the overgrown backyard to see what we wanted. One carried a machete and the other a distrusting stare. Machete man walked up and swung the jumbo knife with an "Ugh" and stuck it in the trunk of the tree next to me. Too, too next to me.

"Hello, we are glad you moved into the neighborhood. Here's some pie we made, just wanted to be neighborly and see if you all needed any help getting settled in." I think we said something like that. The video loop in my mind only caught what they were doing out of mixed emotions of fear for what might happen next and a curious amusement at observing humans in the raw.

Without thanking us, the dad took the pie inside while machete man impressed us with his plans of going out and finding some babes. With his manners, I could not imagine him attracting even the kind still in diapers. He also boasted about having to brave the many enemies of nature to go back into the jungle and find the stepladder they had thrown out there. I could not figure what he meant by that. Maybe I wasn't supposed to.

Anyway a moment later, dad came out with forks. "Ah," I thought, "they are civilized." He plopped the pie down on the kids' little picnic table and told them to have pie. Like flies on cow manure, they descended on that pie, digging holes with their forks.

Machete man realized he did not get a fork so he reached in and grabbed a handful. He stuffed it in his mouth before heading back out to hunt the savage stepladder. I guess he never knew his real ladder.

Dad was already gone into the bush, too. Mom still hid her beach-themed outfit behind the open grill and the conversation was over. As we climbed into our vehicle dumbstruck, she peeked out to yell thank you.

I hope we caught those fine folks at a random moment and that is not how they always live. They moved away shortly afterward. The art of finding favor is not something we are born with, we have to learn it.

We find favor by being merciful and gracious to others. I learned to say, "I understand" to people and then had to learn how to. I discovered that when I look through someone else's perspective, I understand them better. Holding faults destroys relationships. Bragging about yourself will destroy as well.

Build favor by being honest. People hate a liar. Truth came by Jesus,[238] honesty builds "favor and high esteem in the sight of God and man."[239] Jesus is wisdom in the flesh. Even at an early age, He put the principles of Proverbs into action. We must grow not only physically, but also in favor with man and God.

In the school systems, students often lack a sense of the end result of their behavior because they have grown dependent on approval from others. They follow their peers without considering the destructive end results of their attitudes and actions. Short-term acceptance will cause a youth to go drinking with friends, for example.

Isolating groups by age or other classifications destroy social continuity. Individualism also blurs the sense of how one's behavior will affect others or one's self down the road. Jesus does not train His followers in isolation. We work together and stay involved with others.

---

[238] See John 1:14.
[239] Proverbs 3:3-4, NKJV. See also I Samuel 2:26; 3:1-19.

RAISING UNIQUENESS

D O YOU WISH some things had been done differently in the way you were raised? Few tasks demand as much from you as parenting does. I believe my parents had many challenges, and I was one of them.

How about raising children while depending on hearing aids? Come to think of it, that might be the best time of life. I could tune out some things. Anyway, you never plan to bring up a child while leaning on a cane or walker. That doesn't mean it cannot be done.

Mary and Joseph were not the only intentional parents; Elizabeth and Zachariah were, too. If Jesus was a city boy (a rural town, anyway), then John was a country boy. Zack and Liz raised John to also be strong in spirit. This couple, like Abraham and Sarah, show that late-in-life parents and grandparents can do an effective job raising children.

The Lord said that he knew Abraham would raise "his children and his household after him" to "keep the way of the Lord."[240] Zack and Liz heard from the Lord what their child needed. The angel had told him that John would be a great man for the Lord, would not drink any form of alcohol, and would be

---

[240] Genesis 18:19, NKJV.

filled with the Spirit from the womb.[241] "And the child grew and became strong in spirit. And he was in deserted places until the day of his showing to Israel."[242] John had a different upbringing according to his needs and purpose.

The only glimpse we have of Jesus's youth tells us about trips to the big city and hints that He laid block or chiseled stone alongside Joseph.[243] John's history indicates he was more of a loner—he was to become an outspoken witness to the Light of the world.[244] His father was a priest and his mother came from the line of Aaron the first high priest. John's home life was different than that of Jesus, whose parents' ancestry came from King David.

You should not raise two children the same way. Each one has different interests, strengths, and personal traits. The book of wisdom tells us: "Train up a boy on the opening of his way, even when he is old, he will not turn aside from it."[245] In my book for fathers, *Devotions with Dad: Building Character*, we look at raising children according to their unique purpose.

Mary and Joseph brought Jesus each year to Jerusalem for Passover. This is the time of year and place He would die. John matured in the wilderness—and he was called to be a voice

---

[241] See Luke 1:15.
[242] Luke 1:80, LITV.
[243] The Greek word *tektoñ* used in Mark 6:3 for Jesus and Matthew 13:55 for Joseph indicate a tradesman builder or construction worker. Builders do carpentry, but not only carpentry. There are a lot of sayings and traditions built on the idea of Jesus being a carpenter, but that may not be the case. Sorry. Since the biggest construction project of the time near Nazareth was a city of stone, it is very likely that both Joseph and Jesus were stone builders. For one thing, this kills the image we often see in paintings of a wimpy looking Jesus. Stone masons have to pack some shoulder mass and their arms cannot be wispy. The metaphor is awesome, too, that Jesus is the builder, shaping our lives to fit into the masterful House of God. We are His workmanship (Ephesians 2:10) and are living stones (I Peter 2:5).
[244] See John 1:6-9.
[245] Proverbs 22:6, LITV.

in the wilderness, pulling people away from the religion center and back to true faith in God. How is the Lord steering the children whose lives you influence? Train them in the way they should go.

Before age 7, or at least before adolescence, a child is very programmable. Some have likened the pre-pubescent child to a hypnotized person, easily receiving and obeying suggestions and commands. What childhood imprints are still defining your life today? Have you seen anything so far you would like to unload? "Why aren't you more like your brother?" What were you called by exasperated parents or hateful peers? "Why are you so weird?"

What does the Lord say about you instead? "You are mine and I made you with a great purpose." Pause now if you can, and exchange those lies you believed for the Truth He gives.

Some people tell their kids, "I had to learn from the school of hard knocks. You just gotta learn by experience." These clichés lie to us. Many who tell us to learn the hard way may not actually know what to tell us because their experience was painful and they didn't find clear answers either.

If we were supposed to learn everything by experience, why do we see so many examples in the Gospels of Jesus teaching, correcting, and retraining His students? A teacher is a much safer option than experience. Imagine if we all learned "by experience" to look both ways before crossing the road—we'd all be hit by cars! This is why we must see Jesus and not try to figure out life on our own.

We need to be strong in spirit. Those who see Jesus are maturing in managing their emotions. They look to the future with confidence, discern what is going on in the world, and work to improve the lives of those around them.

We see this example in Jesus who spoke articulately to men of the scrolls. He saw clearly that His life was more than that tall white building in Jerusalem. Our Teacher will show us how to be that person. We are seeing Him better as we proceed.

REVEALING LIGHT

EVER FEEL LIKE YOU HAD a purpose but weren't sure what it was? Look at one man's life and you will understand yours better. God, the Light, sent a person: "his name was John."[246]

We only want to see Jesus. So, why must we look at this John guy? Isn't he hogging the spotlight? No. John "was not that Light" but came to "witness concerning the Light."[247] The Lord involves a witness who gets the attention of people so they will look at Him.

Our man "J" did not crowd into the spotlight; he turned it on. Imagine watching a stage drama that had no lighting. The main actor stands up to give catchy lines and flash his winning smile. However, no one can see his bleached-white teeth and greased-back hair. There aren't any of those people who run around behind the scenes turning on lights and aiming them correctly.

John served as that behind-the-scenes guy pointing others to Jesus.[248] Let's say a local dealership was giving away Toyota

---

246 John 1:6, LITV.
247 John 1:8, LITV.
248 See John 1:7.

Tundras. They could not help anyone who had not been told to go get their free pickup truck. You and I know about Jesus because someone else helped us see Him. Even if you found out about Jesus only from reading the Gospels, you have humans to thank—the Gospel writers spotlighted Jesus by scratching words on cowhide parchments.

This man John will be the baptizer, preparing the Way for the Lord. He knew he was not the Light.[249] Too many people start bringing attention to Jesus but then decide that rather than aim the spotlight, they want to be in it. We are not the Light. Pretenders want to be the star of the religious show. They want others to think they have it all figured out. Don't be that guy.

In a different but similar way, I have had to learn to not hog the spotlight as a parent. When people compliment my wife and me on our children's looks or their character, it is too easy to want to hog the attention. "Thank you, we are very fortunate to be their parents." Our children are a gift from God and I cannot claim to be the author of any commendable qualities in them.

On another level, when I reached a certain achievement in my writing one day, I felt the lure of sitting back and soaking in the rays for a minute. Rather than poke more feathers in my hat, however, I have learned to keep doing the work that brings attention to Jesus. "Wow, if Jesus hadn't carried me through some hard times, I would not have made it to this point in my writing ministry." Your life will have different specifics but the same challenges. Keep turning that light back on Him.

I had a friend tell me he liked being with me because it made him feel like he was close to God. This saddened me that he did not have access to the Lord for himself. We spent time in the Scriptures and he began to see Jesus for himself. When he let the Spirit of the Lord fill that emptiness in his life, he did not have to depend on another person to feel close to Jesus.

---

[249] See John 1:8.

John brought others' attention to the Light. No one qualifies to shine His light, yet this is the only way He shines it. This light ignites the wick in every human life, but most suppress it and never let the Light from above illuminate their lives.[250] Those who will shine His light, like John did, help others find Him, too.

A friend gave our family a wax-melting pot for putting good scents in the air. A light bulb inside this clay, jar-like container heats up wax in the tray on top. In our active household with young children, it has fallen and broken a few times. Each time, we have glued it back together and keep it working because of sentimental value. Last time, my daughter repaired it with hot glue. Now, you can turn that little bulb on in a dark room and it does more than melt wax; through those cracks, light shines out and brightens the whole room.

I may not understand why the Lord limited the Light to only shine through humans, but I do see how. We all come to Him with hurts, mistakes, and serious setbacks in life. Those things leave us broken and somewhat misshapen. Rather than be worthless, the Light can now shine through those rough places in our lives.

Are you ashamed of where your life had to be glued back together? Have you tried to hide the scars from those times you shattered? I want you to know that if you will see Jesus, others will see Him through you. The better He shines in you, the more He will shine to others.

In the rough and hostile wilderness, John prepared for shining the Light. The wounds and disappointments in your wilderness of life have been preparing you to shine. We get to help those in darkness see the Light. Let the creation see the Creator in a whole new angle.

---

[250] See John 1:9.

God has sent you where you are to be a witness. You live in the home you have because someone in darkness needs to see. Maybe you took a job because you thought you had bills to pay. Your relatives, your school, your church, your neighborhood, and the places you spend money are looking at you. We are Light leakers.[251] Without your brokenness, they would never see the Light inside you.

---

[251] See I John 4:14.

A MESSAGE OF CHANGE

MANY STORIES BEGIN "Once upon a time in a land far, far away." We do not believe those stories. They are fairy tales. This story will also not end with "they all lived happily ever after" either.

Luke gives us only the best details from the Jesus biography. He studied all available facts and put together the most resourced production on the life of the Messiah.[252] The opening credits have rolled past. The "Directed by" title has faded away. Let the seeing begin!

Luke pans from the Emperor of Rome to the governor of Judea (southern Israel), the ruler of Galilee (northern Israel), then the rulers of the surrounding territories, and then the high priests in Jerusalem.[253] People in Luke's day knew these players by name. Luke puts Preacher John right up there with those important names.

Society should recognize God's messengers as well as they do politicians and celebrities. Within the founding documents of the United States, you can find exact phrases from contemporary sermons in the American colonies. Preachers influenced the

---

[252] See Luke 1:1-4.
[253] See Luke 3:1-2.

foundations of the USA. Separation of church and state should only be a one-way concept. The State should not control the Church, but the Church must influence the State.

Young people tend to dress and act like the celebrities of our day and adopt their views on life. If they could see God's spokespeople as more important, this world would be different. How did Zack and Liz raise John to want to be a preacher? John grew up in a line of priests—those dedicated to serving the Lord. He grew up wanting to be like men like Moses and Zadok. Maybe he had a signed poster of Elijah on his wall. That star preacher wore an animal-skin robe with a leather belt. John dressed like his hero.[254]

John was not a young person looking for meaning in entertainment. He had a purpose. The Spirit that filled him in the womb made the difference. As a teen, I fought the same challenges as anyone else. That same Spirit working on John also kept me through those years, though I was not filled while in the womb.

John had a calling and purpose in the Lord—his parents knew that long ago. One day the word of God came to this priestly man in the wilderness. Moses received the commandments in a wilderness. Elijah heard the whisper of God's voice in the wilderness, too.

John was not some eccentric babbling in the bush but a man of power. From this wilderness, previous generations of Jewish heroes led guerilla attacks against Greek forces. Out of your dusty wilderness, too, you will find strength for your mission.

John came preaching to people who should have been serving the Lord. He told them to turn from sin. He plunged them underwater to make them clean in the sight of the Lord.[255]

---

254 See II Kings 1:8 and Matthew 3:4.
255 See Luke 3:3.

This memorable act of obedience became a powerful step in turning from the old way. Usually, only Gentile converts to Judaism immersed in water. When John told the Jews (covenant people descended from Abraham) to "wash" like this, He placed them on the level of those who did not know God.

Typically, we call this man "John the Baptist."[256] We realize that John the Baptist never saw a Baptist church (which did not appear for another millennium and a half). So why is this term "Baptist" after his name? It comes to us from French and Latin which got it from the Greek root for "*Baptistēs*" and "*baptizo.*"[257]

When you hear the word "baptize" you probably think of a scene in a church building with someone getting wet. But those who heard the original Greek word did not think that. To them, the word was used for immersing or washing objects. The simple translation of that root word would have been "to immerse, plunge, or wash." At the time of the English translations, a very thick "filter" from a prevailing religious institution declared that baptism did not mean to immerse but that it could mean sprinkling or pouring. Since this was not an English word, people accepted however the religion pros defined it.

Does it shock you that there would be a filter like this in the Bible? Don't worry; there is no problem here with the Bible, just our English translations. I grew up reading the *King James Version* and love that text. Some Bible translations filter out important elements we need to see.[258] Another carry-over word is "Christian." I wish it had been translated as the original hears

---

[256] Matthew 3:1.
[257] Meaning "to immerse, dip, or plunge."
[258] This of course does not mean that it is wrong to use a translation and we all have to learn the original languages. Even Jesus and the writers of the New Testament appear to have used Greek translations as well as quotes from the original Hebrew. We need to be aware of the agenda of any Bible translation and thoroughly research to be sure we are not being blindsided.

would have understood it: "anointed ones." We will address that idea more in the next book.

A correct translation might have us call this man "John the Plunger." He could have also been labeled "The Big Dipper." Given the other connotations of those words, neither of those seem respectful of the man and his role. Maybe his listeners thought of him as "John the Washer" which not only fits the uses of that word but also his actions in the washing of sin in the Jordan.

To keep us looking through a clear lens with no filter, I will often refer to him as John the Immerser or at least John the Baptizer. John was plunging people under water in the Jordan River as both the original word and the surrounding contexts make clear. We will look at that more in a moment.

John did not snap any filters on the truth. The command that they "Repent!"[259] did not give the listeners any options. This means to turn from going the wrong way and head toward the Lord.

Too much church preaching today does not carry this message. Instead, many TV preachers say stuff more along the lines of, "Your problems are not your fault and we are here to help you feel better about yourself." It seems that same tune flows through talk shows and other humanistic programs on the tube.

Since we mentioned celebrating preachers, we have to recognize that they are not all on par with John. We should celebrate a preacher who helps set people free from sin and doesn't bandage their guilt about it. The criers of old would demand that the people of Israel turn from sin when they would wander away from the Lord. John came in a long line of yelling servants who turned people back to God.

---

[259] Matthew 3:2.

What was not part of the tradition was John's clear message for people to prepare their hearts because the "Kingdom of Heaven" had come near.[260] This sounded like a new message. What kind of Kingdom would this be? How was Heaven's Nation different from the Kingdom of Israel? John has announced a new era on earth.

In the countryside around the Jordan River, John had a bulldozer ministry. He traveled around the Jordan valley, getting the people to turn back to the God their ancestors had served.[261] He may have seemed back-woodsy in many ways, but he was influential.

I would have liked meeting John. He was not your suit-and-tie kind of preacher. He was a tough dude, living off the grid, eating gluten-free, organic, free-range, wild-caught diet. Okay, insects. He ate insects: locusts. He also ate insect spit: honey.[262]

According to some, eating certain insects can be very healthy.[263] If you must eat some, try dipping them in honey as John did. Better yet dip them in chocolate—I'm sure he would have if he'd known of it. He'd probably have made his coffee over the campfire and strained it through a sock, too.

The people who argued with his dad about what to name him were also upset to see him living in his van down by the river like this. Okay, I'm just kidding. He did not have a van. A truck. I can see him in the bed of a truck, looking at the night sky, talking to God. However he lived, there were those who talked in hushed tones about him.

"That man should have been a priest like his father."

"I know it. What happened?"

---

[260] Matthew 3:2.
[261] See Luke 3:3.
[262] See Mark 1:6.
[263] See the research of Dr. Weston Price on the benefits of eating insects.

"Can't say. He's been different since before he was born. They say he could sense stuff even when he was in the womb."

"I heard he got caught up with that group out there by the Dead Sea."

"That cult with the vow of poverty out there hiding Scripture scrolls? Then why isn't he living with them? Once you are in that group, you can never leave."

"Maybe he's recruiting members."

"Nah. He is out there talking about a new kingdom."

"Do you think he plans to restart the true line of priests again?"

"I don't know. Maybe we should go hear him for ourselves."

To work in the Temple, a priest had to be washed with water.[264] A priest would also immerse certain Temple tools and utensils in water to make them pure and dedicated for use before the Lord.[265] John immersed humans as instruments for the eternal Temple, cleansing them like as priests for the Lord's service in the new Kingdom.

Where did John get his message of repentance from? Isaiah prophesied that a man would come, yelling in the wilderness, equalizing every high thing and every low thing, straightening out what was crooked and smoothing the rough places.[266] He preached that people should turn and the waywardness had to stop.

---

[264] See Exodus 29:4.
[265] See Mark 7:4. This practice shows how the Pharisees carried the Temple ritual into everyday practice.
[266] See Isaiah 40:3-5; Luke 3:3-6.

When construction crews came to build a freeway in our corner of Missouri, we heard the roar of huge dozers and watched loaders drive through our Ozark hills. They invested years of work and millions of dollars to get that road leveled and smooth. Earthmovers took the dirt off the tops of the high places and filled in the valleys below. This is the work of the preacher.

You cannot bring people to God if they want to continue in their twisted lives. A message of hope must come with the command of what we must do to access it. For the Lord to travel among us, we need our jagged edges knocked off. Give the Lord your rough spots so He can work in your life.

Isaiah said "All flesh shall see it together,"[267] meaning Gentiles would, too. No one is closer to the Lord than another. Jews are not ahead of non-Jews; the rich are not ahead of the poor; everyone shares common ground. What will everyone see? The salvation of God, which is Jesus!

John's life and message moved huge numbers of people. They came from the area around to confess their sins and be immersed by him.[268] A significant renewal movement develops when something begins to draw people. They did not know what they were drawn toward, but soon we will see that they wanted to see Jesus, whether they knew it or not.

God's people must obey the command to repent. Sometimes you need to turn from your religion. Some people in religious ruts struggle with the same issues they had when they first came to the Lord. Masks of good behavior do not bring lasting change inside.

When those already-religious people came streaming out to John, they changed their thinking, "confessing their sins."[269] Many religious people have convinced themselves they don't

---

[267] Isaiah 40:5, LITV.
[268] See Matthew 3:5; Mark 1:5.
[269] Mark 1:5, LITV.

have wrongdoing they need to admit. By seeing and confessing where we are wrong, we prepare our hearts to see Jesus.

Why did the Lord send someone yelling in the wilderness? The religious buildings made little room for Him. Today, too, God has to work outside of many church buildings to get anything done.

In the next chapter, we look at how to be sure we don't get stuck in self-validating ritualism. Right now, defeat that spirit of religious pride by confessing your sins to the Lord. Ask for His help as you turn from the old path.

MAKE IT LEGIT

BLUE AND ORANGE SUNLIGHT STREAMED through the stained-glass windows as I wiped tears from my eyes. In my mid-teens, I was struggling with figuring out who I was. There, in a chapel decorated with old-school Bible scenes, I saw Jesus.

I don't remember what the Jesus in that glass looked like. I was not looking at the glass. In fact, I was looking at... a clown.

Before this moment, I had spent years trying to be a clown for Jesus. I had learned to juggle clubs, ride a unicycle, and breathe through a plastic red nose. That week was a kids' camp and a clown was doing the preaching and stuff. If you haven't heard a clown preach, your religion needs help, that's all I'm saying.

The King's Clown, Lloyd Squires, had involved me in a parade through that chapel and some other songs and fun stuff for the kids. I hit a crisis while trying to wear neon and polka dots. This was not me.

I climbed upstairs to the empty balcony to hide, think, and deal with what I felt. As the King's Clown talked to the younger set that day, Jesus began to pull on my heart. I choked back tears, and then I didn't. It felt like my heart was being ripped out of my chest. Yet it felt good.

Jesus showed me His plan for me was not a red nose but a pen,... a word processor,... ink on paper. He wanted me to write for Him. At that moment He confirmed and clarified so much and re-aimed my life.

Even if you don't call yourself religious, you already have your ideas about Jesus. Anyone mature enough to read this has formed some mental idea of who this Man is. I'm glad you have heard about Him, but preconceived ideas can be a problem. Our best impressions of Jesus could be no better than looking through stained glass.

Later, I returned to walk the aisle of that chapel when I completed my graduate studies in theology. While I loved learning from books and had wonderful teachers, it took me some time to get away from my religious geekiness to enter a friendship with Jesus.

I am not serving a Jesus of the stained glass. No doubt, stained glass was the hip thing in its day, but I notice something the artists probably didn't intend. That warbled glass forces you to look at it rather than through it. Someone could be standing on the other side of the colorized window pane and you might not recognize their facial features.

Physical windows are not limiting our vision, but spiritual ones are. Many people see Jesus through a windowpane of a religious tradition which looked great when it was new. After you slide those windows out of your way, or completely shatter them, the Jesus you see will take your breath away.

People who do not know Jesus might see the Jesus of the church house, a Jesus of the TV preacher, a Jesus of the political cause, or another Jesus through some other warbled lens. The purpose of this book (and the ones that follow in this series) is to open the window and see Him in 20/20 vision. No spectacles, no trifocals, no blindfolds, no manmade glass, just Jesus.

John encountered people who only looked through "stained glass." They joined forces against his message. We are not talking here about personal perspectives or optional religious points of view. Wrong perspectives on Jesus war against the right view of Him. This started before He stepped into the spotlight and you are the prize they are fighting for.

Every thesis has an antithesis. Every pasta has an antipasto (okay, maybe not). Every hero has a villain. Our hero is Jesus, but who is the "bad guy"? You might be surprised.

Matthew's cinematography brings new actors onto the screen of our minds: Pharisees and Sadducees. These were the religion professionals of the day. Don't hate them for that. Yet.

It all started out good, like most denominations and church movements. A Sadducee ("Sad, you see") believed that the Temple should be ruled by those of the true line of Zadok, an important high priest from Israel's golden age when King David ruled. Beyond bloodline, which was hard to prove anyway, this group focused on life here and now, playing politics, and competing for control. Their influence and focus centered mainly on Jerusalem.

The other group, called "Pharisees," also serves as a foil to Jesus in the Gospels. They impressed and influenced many of the common people. They had begun not as a power preservationist movement like the Sadducees, but as a restoration movement for keeping *Torah*.

The Pharisees' goal was to stir Israel up to return to living by the code of Moses so that the Messiah could come. They prayed, talked about life after death, fasted, and lived with strict discipline. Eventually, their belief system became about themselves rather than pure-hearted devotion to the Lord.

We will get to know these guys better as we travel the dusty paths from Jerusalem to Galilee. John already knew them too well. When he preached to the Pharisees and Sadducees, he did not say, "Well, look! It is so nice to have the local ministerial alliance representing tonight." Nah. No polished ecumenicalism with John.

He said, "Offspring of vipers! Who warned you to flee from the wrath to come?"[270] Imagine a preacher today giving a shout out to other religion professionals in the crowd, "Look, we have the sons of serpents here with us tonight. What did you come here for? Trying to find a way out of the judgment you deserve?" I think I would fall out of my chair laughing if that happened.

John might have said this to me, too.

[Gets back in chair.]

John also said this to the crowds of people in the area under the spell of those "experts."[271] Were they coming because they wanted to escape God's judgment, or were they just looking for the next religious circus to attend? What about you? I know I have chased religious fads before. I think John would have yelled at me during those phases of my life.

Leaders who controlled Jerusalem caught wind of what was happening in the country. The Sadducees had to dispel uprisings among the people or Rome would take away their authority at the Temple. They became wet blankets to any spiritual wildfires that might arise. John knew that. These priestly folks were his people after all.

A religious spirit at work in our world today doesn't want you to become too passionate. "Be religious, but keep it hush," they say. "Don't be emotional. Don't be driven." Yet you are here because you want to be like John.

John's fiery and focused preaching attracted a large group of followers in a short time. He called out the ones who just came for the show. John was not trying to start a megachurch.

He did not call them generic snakes, but vipers. Vipers would bite and suck blood during the night. Some religious

---

[270] Matthew 3:7, LITV.
[271] See Luke 3:7.

153

people get their energy from sucking the life out of unsuspecting people. The first serpent we read about in history got Eve and Adam to eat the forbidden fruit. John calls them "offspring of serpents," or agents of Satan.

John did not tell them to leave. Though his words were strong, he was not telling them, "Get outta here!" He did not wimp out from addressing the issues, calling them to a change of mind and heart. I don't suggest that you talk to the next person you see this way. Strong words like this are for those whose hard hearts have blinded them.

"Bring forth fruits worthy of repentance."[272] John yanked at their blindfolds. In effect, he was telling them to produce changes in their lives on the same level as their change of heart. We must have this too. Changed thinking changes behavior.

John would have laughed at the idea of selling a signature Bible like religious celebs do today. There go his groupies with gold-edged copies of the "John the Plunger Bible" covered with genuine camel-skin. The sales might have given him income enough to have more than bugs to eat. John didn't need customers, just converts.

He called listeners to turn from their sin and stop depending on their religious association. They had racial and religious pride. "We have Abraham as our father," was as exclusive as it sounds. John threw rocks through their stained-glass-encased beliefs, telling them God could create children for Abraham from the stones some were sitting on.[273]

Rocks cannot produce humans, biologically. I'm sure you knew that. So did John's audience, but his illustration told them their pedigree in the flesh meant nothing if they were children of

---

[272] Luke 3:8, LITV.
[273] There is wordplay in Aramaic, the popular sister language to Hebrew that most Jews spoke during that time, between the word for "stones" and "children."

the serpent in their hearts. A true child of Abraham believes even though he or she does not see. He accepted God's label for him as "father of a multitude" while he and his post-menopausal wife were childless.

The Jews' success at survival amazed them—they had existed against all attempts at extermination. They knew they were unique and had a different place on the planet than others. Some Christians gloat like this, too. Because they think they are the answer, they are not ready to change. Some might say, "But we are preachers." John would answer those in dead religion, "I don't care—God can raise up preachers from your pews."

Some folks put their faith in their faith, attending church services out of pride. The religious traditionalists came to John to get validated or almost as if to get a promotion. They should have come to humble themselves.

John calls these descendants of Abraham to immersion in water for the cleansing of their sins. They found it insulting. He found it necessary. He could have said, "Wow, look at this large following!" Instead, in his method, the weak believers get culled, not called. How different this is from modern methods which depend on numbers to measure success.[274]

Your tree is about to come down, John says.[275] Israel had wandered away as a whole nation. The Sadducees were not devoted to the Lord but to their control of the Temple, being more political than prophetic. The Pharisees, after a few generations of being a revival movement, were just holding onto their name and ritual identity. Nothing but firewood there.

If you ran a commercial orchard and the apples tasted nasty, you wouldn't repaint the tree. If you couldn't improve the

---

[274] Not that it is wrong to count or keep records. The real issue is what we are counting. Only devoted people count for Kingdom purposes.
[275] See Matthew 3:10; Luke 3:9.

fruit, you would have to cut the root. If you will not examine your life's fruit, you will not know if you need to change. A corrupt tree must come down. You throw the whole thing out.

Religious traditionalists have the hardest time seeing that they need a total overhaul. They think they need improvements rather than total replacement. They think themselves better than gangsters and druggies.

Trees stand out, obvious above all the other landscape. The religious power brokers towered high and mighty like trees. John's bulldozer must take down trees that get in the way, pile them up, and let them burn. You cannot build a highway of holiness and let self-righteous trees stay standing.

A faithful church member could live in hidden sin (bad fruit) and think it is no big deal. But the Lord is in the clear-cutting business. He will mow down deceitful religious people and add them to His bonfire.

True Kingdom work speaks to sin and demands its removal. John challenged hard hearts. It takes a heavy blow to get through a thick skull. His harsh words are not how we approach everyone.

John did not beg, "Please join this thing." He as much as said, "You better prove that you are committed to this cause."

If you want to go to college, you must pass a college entrance exam. The school wants you there—that is why they spend so much money on billboards and scouts. Still, you cannot enter until you show you take learning seriously. Not only do they need your tuition money and enrollment, but they need you to represent them well afterward. They do not want to be known as the school that graduates lazy brains.

Entering the Kingdom is like taking a college entrance exam. The Kingdom does not allow just anyone to come in, although all are invited. In that invitation is an application. Of course, this does not negate the free gift, but to get that full scholarship, we prove we are committed. No school wants to enroll a non-committed squad who drop out later.

The ones stirred by this no-nonsense preacher come and ask, "What should we do?"[276] John gives them the entrance exam. Their résumé needs to include generosity, self-control, kindness, and contentment, to name a few.[277]

John does not lay down these stipulations because he is building his own group. These heart-drives align us with Jesus. I have heard many say, "Just come to Jesus as you are." John did not say that. He explained the prep work we need to do to be ready for Jesus. Aren't you glad you didn't skip these opening credits now?

Do you have two of something? John said we must give one to the person who doesn't have one.[278] Think of the changes contained in that command: from greed to kindness, from selfishness to selflessness, from hoarding to helping. Start with these prereqs if you wish to enroll in the school from above. Got food? Share it. Don't just feed yourself.

The tax collectors of then might have given you the same feel as bill collectors might today. Tax collectors included those who charged customs dues or toll fees to travelers. Most people hated them because they abused their authority to make themselves rich, as do many government officials today. John said not to take more than necessary.[279]

Do you take advantage of your occupation or official role in something? Do you demand more from people than they should have to pay or force more work from them than is fair? Kindness is key to the Kingdom.

---

[276] Luke 3:10, paraphrased. This is a powerful indicator of a repentant heart. This foreshadows the question in Acts 2:37 that prompts the groundbreaking response from a later preacher.
[277] See Luke 3:11-14.
[278] See Luke 3:11.
[279] See Luke 3:13.

Rome, like most countries, employed soldiers. Those military men often used brute force for selfish reasons. During peace times, they moved among the people similar to our police officers, in some ways. Police brutality must have been an issue then because John called them to not "shake people violently."[280]

Do you use physical force to get what you want? Parents might bully children, husbands might manhandle their wives, or bosses could push their workers around. Those behaviors do not reflect a changed heart.

Some people use their position to intimidate and manipulate others. John calls down those who accuse others falsely. Soldiers could get away with a lot, such as forcing citizens to carry their gear for them. If you accused someone who was not a Roman citizen, they would not have much voice in court and you could take advantage. This might include claiming someone was guilty of stealing something so you could seize it for yourself.

The King does not work like that, so neither do those who follow Him. Why would a military person take something that did not belong to him? Because of the universal problem we have with people feeling like they deserve more.

Also to the soldiers, John says, "Be content with your wages."[281] Memes circle the internet comparing the huge gap between the wages of US military veterans and the income of US Senators. John would not have approved of such memes. He probably would say, "You agreed to that wage when you enlisted, why complain now?" This concept of contentment speaks to us all, military or not.

Have you ever gotten a bonus or a raise and you said, "This is too much. I don't need all that money"? I didn't think so. Like the maggot, we always crave to consume more. Those who

---

[280] See Luke 3:14, LITV.
[281] See Luke 3:14.

do not want to be chopped down by the ax stop living for self. We should not think of ourselves as entitled to anything.

Generous, considerate people show they are ready to see Jesus. This is not earning access to Jesus, but preparation. Later, you will see Jesus require the same change of dynamics before legitimizing new followers.

The Kingdom-entrance exam asks, "Do you care about others? Do you make people feel the way you want to feel? Are you contented or greedy?" What do you need to do before you would qualify for John to baptize you?

Everyone has changes to make and wrongs to right when they come to the Lord. What does your fruit look like? Be generous not because you should but because you care about others. Changed actions reveal a changed heart. What changes do you see in yourself?

Why is generosity one of the tests in this entrance examination? Because gracious people receive grace. Harsh people do not find favor with the Lord very well. Hateful people will make a bad name for the loving King. If you give a cold drink of water to the thirsty, you are close to the Kingdom.

Common people, government workers, and military personnel asked, "What should we do?" Did you notice who did not ask? Where were the Pharisees and Sadducees John preached to? The religion pros were not asking, not seeking to change.

Traditional Jews thought of Jewish tax collectors and soldiers as traitors because they were supporting their Roman enemies instead of Israelite sovereignty. Those undesirable "traitors" show up early in the narrative as role-models for us because their hearts opened to healthy change.

So, we have mentioned religious pride and pointed out people who justify themselves by their religious behavior. It is the tendency in all of us to feel okay because we do the right things. Reading my Bible, attending church, and praying faithfully are all good things, but could my level of commitment blind me to what is really in my heart?

Where did John's message hit you? Grumbling about your income? Holding onto extras things instead of giving to those who don't have much? Bullying someone with force or manipulation? Being thoughtful to people who cannot pay you back?

What will you do? Hide behind stained glass? Or humble your heart and change your ways?

Do something solid this week in keeping with your changed heart. Give away that second pair of shoes, or ask your boss to forgive you for always hinting that you want a bigger paycheck. Let this be the beginning of deep changes in you.

SETTING THINGS RIGHT

JOHN THE BAPTIZER was a mechanic doing spiritual realignments. The vehicle called "Israel" had gotten off track. If you have taken your car in for front-end work, you know that once the mechanic wrenches creaky bolts around for a while and greases the joints, the steering feels so right.

Traveling through the gospels realigns the direction of my faith. Misaligned cars are not evil, just victims of the wear and tear of the journey. Decent people get thrown off course at times. I have done intensive studies of the Gospels a few times and each trip adjusts the torque on major parts of my life.

Do you want the preacher from the wilderness to change your life? How about putting aside all the other distractions while we take this journey together? If you could remove the notifications from the social apps on your phone, put the cable subscription on pause for a while, and remove any other distractions, you will be able to see parts of your morals that have gotten loose and sloppy. I know we think we need those conveniences we have today, but what if you took a break from entertainment and amusement for an intense focus on Jesus for at least a week?

How about a month?

Brace yourself! This realignment will not be easy. Having to discard well-worn parts of yourself might hurt. Getting on the right track of the King's Highway will be worth the temporary adjustment.

Have you ever had a broken screen door flapping on your house? It might have cost some money and been a pain to fix it, but afterward, it is so nice to sit down inside and enjoy the quiet. That is the settled feeling of correction, the joy of your world being in order.

The whole countryside was coming out to John. His followers were coming from as far as 90 miles away. He was a great leader. So great, the people begin to think he was the promised One who would bring Israel to victory over all the earth.[282]

John rejects their claim. He came to introduce the lesser work of water immersion. Though this step is necessary for those who want to be right with God, a greater work comes with the One for whom he has been bulldozing.

Of the Strong One who was coming, John the Washer said, "I am not fit to loosen the thong of His sandals."[283] Apparently, tradition said that a rabbi should not force a follower to tie his sandals. Only the lowest slave did that kind of work. John makes it clear that he does not qualify to do even the most insulting of jobs for this coming One.

When an emcee (MC) introduces the next speaker, audiences have more respect for that person. Image your favorite preacher saying, "I met a great preacher." You would want to hear the great speaker because of that recommendation from the someone you highly admired. Knowing how dynamic his ministry was, John used his influence to bring attention to Jesus as so much greater. His slave/sandal visual shows them that the

---

[282] See Luke 3:15.
[283] Luke 3:16, LITV.

One following John's introduction was at least a hundred times greater than John.

Ask any Christian why Jesus came and I imagine 99% would give you the wrong answer. John announced Jesus. Either the main speaker does what is claimed about them, or the emcee is a liar. John was not a liar, but so many religious people do not listen to him. They ignore John and assume they know why Jesus came.

John said, "He will immerse you in the Holy Spirit."[284] John introduced water immersion; Jesus introduced Spirit immersion. There goes another mask over the truth. I am shocked at how many groups call themselves Christian when they are not even aware of this key purpose behind Jesus's arrival.

Every one of the Gospel books introduces Jesus as coming to baptize—fully immerse, not just sprinkle—you and me with the Spirit. Are you living a Spirit-immersed life? Prior to Jesus coming, Scripture records the Spirit working through those who would prophesy, work for the Lord, or serve Him as king. You are to be saturated with the Spirit because you are royalty, a priest, and a prophet!

If you consider yourself Spirit-filled, reflect on that idea for a moment. Are you a Spirit-baptized person or a Spirit-immersed person? A simple return to biblical thinking will help reshape the way we live.

As a child, I remember the distinct moment the Spirit of God came into my life. I am thankful for my mother's prayers helping trigger that powerful experience. However, only in young adulthood did I realize what it meant to be immersed in the Spirit. As a child, I didn't know how much I needed a Spirit-soaked life. Jesus did not come to splash us with the Spirit's fruit of love and joy but to saturate us!

---

[284] See Matthew 3:11 and Luke 3:16.

163

The crier also said that Jesus comes to "gather His wheat into the storehouse."[285] Wheat comes in a plain brown wrapper called the hull. Workers would thresh the wheat by beating it[286] and the hulls would break loose from the wheat kernels. Using a sifting fan[287] (something like a wicker shovel), they scooped up the grain and tossed it into the air. The wind would then blow away hulls, any leaves, and straw (the chaff). Then they stored the grain in the barn.

John's illustration of Jesus gathering the wheat parallels his previous illustration of Jesus immersing with the Spirit. Those He baptizes in the Spirit He separates out for keeping in God's eternal storehouse. The "baptism of fire" then parallels the burning of the chaff. While the term "baptism of fire" has been used by Christians to speak of having a zeal for the Lord, John's immediate context shows that the chaff gets destroyed. We want to be the ones who enter the Kingdom, the storehouse.

Chaff is not thorns or weeds, so this illustration is not just about bad people. Chaff is the hulls, useless byproducts left over after the wheat harvest. Is John saying that those who are not productive will be thrown into the fire? Either the Spirit consumes and empowers you, or you are consumed by worthlessness and destroyed. Jesus came to bring hope[288] and judgment.[289] No one can quench or put out the fire He brings.[290]

---

[285] Matthew 3:12, LITV.
[286] They could do this manually with a threshing flail, a tool consisting of two sticks joined by rope which they would swing and strike downward on the pile of freshly harvested grain. In larger operations, an ox would pull a skid or pallet across a whole floor of grain, rolling and releasing the hulls under the weight.
[287] Luke 3:17, LITV. Also called a "winnowing fork."
[288] See Matthew 11:4-5, 25-30.
[289] See Matthew 11:20-24.
[290] See Matthew 25:41; Jude 1:7.

Notice that Jesus will clean the threshing floor completely. A person is either wheat or chaff. There is no middle ground. A person either gets immersed with the Spirit or gets burned. No one will be left behind at harvest time. The wheat-in-the-barn represents eternity with Jesus and the hull-fire warns us of hellfire.

John preached that the chaff and bad-fruit-bearing trees would be thrown into flames. A person is either Spirit-immersed or hell-bound; there are no other options. He will thoroughly purge (cleanse) His floor (earth?).[291]

Spirit baptism does not abolish the need for water baptism and vice versa. One religious filter causes some to say the Spirit filled them when they were water baptized. John did not understand it that way. He gave them water immersion and explained that Jesus was coming to introduce Spirit immersion as a distinct experience (although both can happen together). We will see Jesus teach more on this soon (addressed in my next book).

When John announced Jesus as coming to judge between the two types of humans, He effectively declared Jesus to be God. We might not see this right away, but the Jews understood that no mere mortal can bring judgment like this. Eternal judgment can only be handled by the eternal One. John knew Jesus was exceptional beyond any other rabbi or prophet; thus he was not worthy to touch His sandal strap.

John takes a person by surprise. He comes on so strong it seems like he is angry or harsh. Not at all. The people loved him.[292] You can have a clear and distinct message without being a bully about it.

---

[291] See Matthew 3:12 and Luke 3:17.
[292] See Luke 3:15.

It was not hate-speech for John to say some will make it and some will be burned. If you were sitting on a park bench with dynamite under it, would it be hateful for me to warn you about it or would you feel loved that I said something? The harsh and condemning voices of some religious people have skewed our thinking to make us feel like we cannot be outspoken without being cruel. We need to relearn how to be distinct without being destructive.

As John continued "exhorting many different things, he preached the gospel to the people."[293] The "gospel" was a form of good news announced publically. The good news in his message was that a new government was coming. The new King would saturate people with what is good, pure, holy. He will treasure, preserve, and not discarded those initiated into His "barn." We have the choice to enter this new realm—good news!

An "evangelist" in the Roman times was a crier who went forth announcing the good news (gospel) of a new emperor's rule. In response to the evangelist's message, people would bow and worship their new king. John proclaims the good news that a new and greatest-ever world Ruler was coming onto the scene.

Imagine if someone told you that the crooked politicians had been drained from the swamp, the national debt paid off, and honest people now held all the public offices. Would that be good news? The gospel of Jesus Christ trumps all that. If we are telling it correctly, many will see and desire this change of order.

In the next chapter, we discover what happens when Jesus comes into full view.

---

[293] Luke 3:18, LITV.

JESUS, IN CLEAR VIEW

WITH THE WIND IN THEIR FACES and sweat on their backs, over a hundred runners hurried forward in Riverside, CA. Given the variety of terrain they had to cover in that footrace, the contestants had to watch out for both their competitors and key landmarks. In the scurry of this NCAA cross-country championship, only Mike Delcavo noticed the proper place to turn.

Pausing to wave to the other runners to follow, he managed to get only four to go along with him. The other 123 missed the sign. "They thought it was funny that I went the right way," Mike said later.[294]

Most Christians are chasing the wrong path. They did not see the signs; they do not know the path. Following traditional ruts can feel like the right way because it looks familiar, but throughout this series, we will repeatedly ask ourselves if we are on the right path in all aspects of life.

Many head together in the wrong direction. It feels right when the majority is with you. Like the runner, John is waving to you and me. He didn't create this path, but he saw it and had to

---

[294] Loren D. Mcbain, "They Thought It Was Funny That I Went the Right Way," *Leadership*, June 1994. Kerux 33891

tell others. You, too, will soon flag down those you care about, "Look! This is the right way to go!"

You want to end up at the right destination; you want your friends to as well. Jesus is the path. If we can see Him and follow Him, we will arrive at the right destination.

While the whole pack of "runners" in Israel headed the wrong direction, John stood as the lone man pointing to the Sign they all missed. John knew the true identity of Jesus and thus "saw" Him before he saw Him. His daddy had taught him, "John, you are going to prepare the way of the Lord God." John heard from the Lord for himself, too.

Before Jesus walked onto the scene, John knew what sign to look for. John's perspective on Jesus was not through the filter of the flesh. He saw Jesus from heaven's point of view. Thus, he could announce that this One who would follow him was actually his Leader.[295]

John had been born six months before Jesus was. To say Jesus was "before me," John knew this One was not just a man.[296] To say that Jesus came first meant He had to be the eternal One made flesh. As the invisible God, He preceded the messenger John. Many religious "runners" have overlooked this fact, among other things.

While baptizing other people,[297] John saw Jesus come walking up.[298] About eighteen years have gone by since the last

---

[295] See John 1:15. Jesus used the phrase "come after" Him when inviting disciples to follow Him as their Rabbi, such as in Luke 9:23. So, when John says that the One who would "come after" him was before him, he is essentially saying, "This Disciple is my Rabbi." Logically, the Rabbi would baptize the disciple, not vice versa. For John to baptize Jesus made the lesser immerse the Greater. It only looked like Jesus was John's follower. But the Lord has been using the policy of great reversal since Jacob and Esau, and even earlier.

[296] John 1:18.

[297] See Luke 3:21.

[298] He had come from Galilee, where He was living. See Matthew 3:13.

record of Jesus. Why did He show up now? Because He had a work to do and now was the time.

Seeing Jesus humble Himself overwhelms John. "I have need to be baptized by You, and do You come to me?"[299] He knew He was coming and that He would be great, but the sight of Him stooping was too much for the emcee. John tries to get out of this, knowing he needs Jesus to be his Rabbi, not vice versa.

Jesus would not let John off the hook. "Permit it to be so now, for thus it is fitting for us to fulfill all righteousness."[300] The devoted Servant would live according to the Scriptural outline of His life. John only encountered Jesus because he was fulfilling what God required of his own life.

By John baptizing Jesus, it looked like Jesus was becoming his follower. The opposite proved true. John had lived a strict and disciplined life in preparation for Jesus, making him one of Jesus's first "disciples."

John, by rights, should have been a priest like his dad.[301] So, why was he not serving in Jerusalem? He had a higher calling.

Jesus's baptism sets Him out as dedicated to a holy purpose. We, too, become consecrated instruments for the Lord's use when washed in repentance. Through immersion into Jesus Christ, our High Priest, we become devoted to serving in the Temple above.[302] We do this to fulfill all righteousness.

I have heard so many crazy beliefs about baptism; more stained glass needs to be shattered here. Some religion pros say baptism makes you a member of a church or that you do it to announce to others that you are now a Christian. Others say baptism is salvation by works, so you don't really have to. I

---

[299] Matthew 3:14, LITV.
[300] Matthew 3:15, NKJV.
[301] Also, his mother was a descendant of Aaron the first high priest.
[302] See Galatians 3:27 with John 12:26 and Revelation 7:15; 22:3.

cannot list all the theories or ideas, but I can return to the original desire God had in designing baptism.

God, through John, required water immersion of people turning from sin or they would be burned in the fire. I want to have the faith of Jesus. Rather than argue away the meaning of baptism or come up with some unbiblical purpose for it, let's accept it the way Jesus did—as fulfilling the perfect plan for our lives.

Scripture states that baptism effectively pardoned the sins of the converts: "John came baptizing in the wilderness and proclaiming a baptism of repentance for remission of sins."[303] The underlying word translated as "remission"[304] carries the idea of being set at liberty from something. People turned away from their rebellion against God, entered the water with John, and the Lord disconnected them from His judgment against them. Yes, water immersion does fulfill all righteousness while preventing all punishment from God!

Jesus apparently came to take the plunge last after John had immersed all the other people one day.[305] John always made sure people qualified before he immersed them. With Jesus, however, John did not feel qualified.

As Jesus prayed, heaven opened. Faith-filled prayers by those devoted to righteousness will open heaven. Standing on Earth, the sky ripped open above Him, and perhaps Jesus viewed the universe, eternity, all past and future in one glimpse.

While we do not know for sure what He saw, we do know what John saw. What looked like a dove came down and landed on Him. Doves are peaceful and gentle (versus representing

_____

[303] Mark 1:4, LITV. See also Luke 3:3.
[304] Greek *aphesis*, meaning to set someone free as if from prison, to forgive or pardon.
[305] See Luke 3:21.

doom like a vulture might). A dove was an approved sacrificial animal in Israel's Temple worship. Jesus would become the accepted sacrifice like the doves Joseph offered for Him thirty years earlier at the Temple.

Noah's giant boat brought the survivors of the flood to a transformed earth over two millennia before John. Noah had sent out a dove to see if they could survive on the land yet.[306] With Jesus's plunge into the water, the dove signifies moving into a new era as well. Noah's dove finally found a clean place to dwell, letting the occupants know it was safe to leave the ark. So, the Spirit, symbolized as a dove, has found a suitable habitation in the man Jesus. When you become immersed in Jesus Christ, you enter a new world!

Let's not mistake this event as being Jesus's first filling with the Spirit. His conception began with the Spirit.[307] He is God-made-flesh. As God-with-us, He is the one in whom the Spirit of God has always dwelt. Later, Jesus will explain this moment as the anointing of the Spirit.[308] Like a king or priest would have been commissioned with oil poured upon him, Jesus was anointed for the work He would do, as both King and Priest.

While Jesus looked up through the sky and the dove descended, the Voice spoke. This young Man had added nearly two decades to His life since His discovery in Jerusalem of being "about My Father's agenda."[309] Now, another confirmation came as the Voice said, "You are My Son, the Beloved; in You I have been delighting."[310]

For thirty years or so,[311] Jesus had walked the earth with a pure heart and a purpose. Now, He received clear confirmation

---

[306] See Genesis 8:8-12.
[307] See Matthew 1:20; also 4:1 and 12:18-21.
[308] Luke 4:18-19; Isaiah 42:1-4; 61:1.
[309] See Luke 2:49.
[310] Luke 3:22, LITV.
[311] See Luke 3:23.

of His identity and it was time to begin the divine mission. Sometimes you have to walk by faith for years before the fulfillment comes. You do not see the plan He has for you until He opens the heavens to you.

When Jesus heard, "You are My Son," John heard: "This is My Son."[312] Two people heard the divine Voice in two different ways! John was told to watch for this moment when the dove came down.[313] This statement confirms to John that he has accomplished his purpose.

Those words from the sky connect two key prophecies about the Anointed One. If you read Psalm 2, you will find a song about the coronation of a king. Faithful students of Scripture saw this same prophecy as also being about the coming King, to whom Yahweh God said, "You are My Son."[314]

Those same scholars also looked for the Servant whom Isaiah prophesied. What they did not realize was that this suffering Servant was also the Messiah they were seeking. These words thundering from above now link both concepts. The Lord said the Servant was the One "in whom My soul delights!"[315] This confirmed that not only was the reigning King also the suffering Servant, but He stood right now dripping wet in the waters of the Jordan.

Expectancy is high. The big moment has come. Next, let's see how real-life plays out just when you think everything is falling into place.

---

[312] Matthew 3:17, LITV.
[313] See John 1:32-33.
[314] Psalm 2:7, LITV.
[315] Isaiah 42:1, LITV. Another aspect of the statement, which we will examine later, is the phrase "Beloved son." This hearkens back to the words concerning Abraham and his son of promise in Genesis 22:2.

JESUS, OUT OF SIGHT

A FTER JESUS ROSE from the Jordan, Luke shows He was "full of the Holy Spirit."[316] This Spirit, appearing innocent and gentle as a dove, "drove Him" into the wilderness.[317] John had developed in the wilderness. Jesus must go here, too, out of public view.

Don't think of your wilderness experiences as negative things. They shape you and prepare you for your purpose. Too many people today want to be in a spotlight instead of a wilderness that can develop them to be one.

Have you ever entered the howling winds of uncharted territory? I don't know what a wilderness looks like in your mind, but in mine, I see colorlessness: no leaf, no green, no fruit, no blossoms. Jews thought of the wilderness as the place where beasts roamed and evicted demons gathered.

Some say if you are right with God, you won't go through bleak experiences—they will all be joyful. Following Jesus

---

[316] Luke 4:1, LITV.
[317] Mark 1:12, LITV. Luke and Matthew both say "led by the Spirit" (Luke 4:1, LITV; Matthew 4:1). Apparently, being led by the Spirit is the same as being driven by the Spirit. Many times the believer will sense this work of the Spirit, too.

though, we see Him in an empty time out in the wild, yet still in the perfect will of God. You will see Jesus out there better than anywhere else.

The people of Israel would tell their children about the time their greatest hero had gone without food for forty days in the wilderness, alone in the presence of the Lord God. That was the ultimate human experience. Here, however, the ultimate Human experienced forty days alone without food in the wilderness in the presence of the devil.

The devil began to tempt Jesus in all aspects of sin that he lures us into.[318] Watch and learn how the devil works. He keeps trying different tactics to get into a person's life. This will help you understand the relentless attacks of the devil on you in the past. Like a cockroach or mouse, he keeps looking for a way to get in and raid your life.

Right after confirmation of His identity, Jesus faces this temptation to destroy it. Being called by the Lord does not make us immune to the devil's attempts to mislead us—it makes us a bigger target. Even if you are a perfect person, you will be tempted.

When hiring a new worker, many employers will put them on probation for a few weeks or months. In the military, the basic training (boot camp) might last eight to twelve weeks and in many corporations, ninety days. This forty-day-drill is like Jesus's "initiation period." Jesus went through that for me so I could come to Him with confidence when I face times of testing.

The devil is the evil, invisible creature dedicated to destroying humans. He knows he cannot stop his death sentence of eternal suffering. Refusing to go there alone, he works to take

---

[318] See Matthew 4:1 and Luke 4:2 with Hebrews 4:15-16.

everyone with him. The last thing he wants is anyone knowing who they are in God's eyes.

While standing there dripping in the Jordan, Jesus had no reason to question His identity: Son of God, Loved One, Delightful Person. Once you hear God's view, you don't need anyone else's. "Forgiven" and "chosen" are what He says about you, and you should never doubt your identity again. But...

First, the devil questions Jesus's identity: "If you are the Son of God."[319] That moment of getting a strong sense of your purpose will be followed later by, "If God loves you,..." or "If you really belong to Jesus,..." Believe the true Voice, not the voice of the untamed.

Jesus could have defended His identity to Satan, but He did not have to. He knew who He was and that was enough. Instead, He responded with Scripture: "It is written."

The devil tempted Jesus with weird bait: "Speak to this stone that it become a loaf."[320] I haven't checked local or national laws where I'm at, but I am sure none of the statutes make it a crime to turn rocks to bread. Is it a sin to make muffins from limestone? John had said the Lord could turn rocks into descendants of Abraham, so... what's the problem? Much was going on in that encounter, including the temptation for Jesus to break His fast.

From this encounter, we see that the devil wants you to obey him in some small things. You don't have to be a pedophile or gangster to miss God's plan; the devil needs you to surrender to his plans only in little things. Pride sneaks into good people's lives this way, turning something for God's glory into a thing for self-exaltation.

---

[319] Luke 4:3, LITV.
[320] Luke 4:3, LITV.

Driven by physical hunger and powered by divine ability, Jesus could have given the command and made breakfast in seconds. Instead, He chose the better thing. "Man shall not live on bread alone, but on every Word of God."[321]

Many devout Jewish boys memorized the Hebrew Bible (our Old Testament) by age fifteen. Being double that age, Jesus knew it all very well. What does your mouth water for? Food or Scripture? God's Words or man's ways?

By Jesus's choice of Scripture in His answer, He focused on the path we must take: every God-breathed word. Are you living by labels others have given you? Or does your very life and identity flow from God's own nature? Will you take a human path or divine?

Life comes from God's mouth. We must turn from our old thinking. Think God's words. Life is not by human tradition.

Self-denial is part of the walk with God. Fasting, the act of going without eating for a spiritual reason, is a good way to discipline ourselves. Jesus set this example at the beginning of His ministry. Rather than seeking just the taste of something marinated, sautéed, or freshly prepared, we should hunger for God's cravings.

Something bugs me about this story in the wilderness. Though people couldn't see the true identity of Jesus, the devil saw Him clearly. The devil is always the deceiver but not always the deceived.

Satan works nonstop to keep people from seeing Jesus. One of the weapons he uses is religious pride. Perhaps you have had your temper flare when someone challenged your religious beliefs. Could that be a manifestation of pride?

---

[321] Luke 4:4, LITV, quoting from Deuteronomy 8:3.

The enemy leverages another tool: humanity's desire for power. Jesus sees all the kingdoms of the world in an instant. The nation of Israel does not have a "very high mountain"[322] and certainly not one that would show all the nations. In this vision, the devil tempted Jesus.

Look out! A vision could be from the devil. After fasting for many days, a person might believe a vision was an answered prayer. Every supernatural experience is not a good thing. Have you ever followed a vision or dream that was not God's plan for your life? If so, how did that work out?

"I will give all this authority and their glory to You, because it has been delivered to me, and I give it to whomever I wish. Then if You worship before me, all will be Yours."[323] Jesus came to rule the earth. This temptation drives at the core of His identity—a quick way to get to the goal with no pain!

Jesus's end game was to rule over all kingdoms of the earth—yet He would not take the shortcut. When showing the kingdoms of this world, the devil offered more than human governments. Unseen authorities work in your nation in rebellion against God. Jesus has come to take over both unseen and seen forces, but He will do that through me and you. About a year into the Gospel journey, we will see Jesus's strategy to overtake these hostile forces region by region.

Jesus did not engage the tempter in a debate. A person could have said, "What? Who says you have all that power?" I would probably have argued with the devil about whether that power was given to him or he stole it from humanity.[324] Jesus did not discuss anything with the enemy.

---

[322] Matthew 4:8, LITV.

[323] Luke 4:6-7, LITV.

[324] In Genesis 1:28, we see that authority over earth was given to humanity. The devil gained authority over the kingdoms of the world by tricking Eve and Adam to submit to him, as Romans 6:16 explains. Today, the wicked one holds sway over the whole world (I John 5:19, NKJV).

Do you dialogue with the devil? Would you have asked, "What do you mean by 'worship'? One knee, or exactly what?" We should not dialogue with temptation: "What might happen if I tried?" Don't try to outthink your temptation. "It probably isn't all that wrong and God will forgive me."

Jesus had a brilliant mind—even as a child He could stump all the scholars—yet He doesn't try to stump Satan. He stops him: "Go behind me, Satan! For it has been written: 'You shall worship the Lord your God, and Him only you shall serve.'"[325] Speak God-Word.

The real issue at hand was how to get authority. Satan has followers today who literally worship Him. Famous hip-hop artists, businessmen, and movie stars partake in séances, blood-drinking rituals, and even human sacrifice.[326] And, for a time, the enemy delivers on his promises of money and power, but he will collect his fee.

Without dramatically worshipping Satan, many make him lord in many small areas. What do you worship? Wealth and prosperity? Fame and success? What do you hold up as more important than anything else? People cannot see Jesus because of their false focus: "the god of this age has blinded the thoughts of the unbelieving, so that the brightness of the gospel of the glory of Christ who is the image of God, should not dawn on them."[327]

Temptations focus on self-interest. Jesus entered the wilderness for self-denial. Some people serve God out of

---

[325] Luke 4:8, LITV, from Deuteronomy 6:13.
[326] The devil still tempts people to worship him today. There are many such reports about celebrities, entertainers, and politicians. See also books by Rebecca Brown such as *Unbroken Curses* and *He Came to Set the Captives Free*. The devil offers money, fame, and power in exchange for one's soul. Magicians, preachers, and many more have done "miracles" to get rich and powerful through deception.

[327] II Corinthians 4:4, LITV.

witchcraft motives, as in, "If I do this, God will make me happy and give me stuff." Jesus responded as we all must: to serve Him, not make Him serve us.

We also submit ourselves to God (and His Word) and resist the evil one.[328] How did Jesus know this vision was not a godly vision? Easy answer. Someone other than God would be worshiped for it to happen. Everything we do should bring glory to God.[329]

Not to be beaten at his game, the devil resorts to using Scripture, too, like Jesus.[330] Of course, the satanic use of Scripture twists it for selfish interest. Many speakers and writers of "Christian" books are led by Satan to twist Scripture to say what selfish or sinful people want to hear.

The devil knows the Bible. Know it better than he does and know how to use it to God's best interest, not your own. Selfish handling of the Scriptures does harm, not good.

Again questioning Jesus's identity ("If you are the Son of God"[331]), the devil challenges Jesus to jump off the highest point of the Temple in Jerusalem. The back of the sixty-foot-tall Temple overlooked a steep ravine where a body would smash if thrown from that height. This would test God's promises that said the angels would protect Him.[332]

The idea behind this temptation seems to have been that by jumping from the top of the Temple, Jesus could gather a crowd of onlookers who would have been amazed that He didn't die. Satan lured Him to test out all the power He had available as God in flesh. Just because something says "nonflammable fabric"

---

[328] See James 4:7.
[329] See I Corinthians 10:31.
[330] See Luke 4:10-11.
[331] Luke 4:9, LITV.
[332] See Psalm 91:11-12.

does not mean you throw it in the campfire. You do not test the floatation ability of the lunch cooler by throwing it into the river.

Jesus didn't say, "I'm being tempted, someone pray with Me. I need to go on a fast to overcome this—wait, I'm on a fast." He resisted it: "You shall not tempt the Lord your God."[333] This seems pretty simple!

He could have said some smart-mouthed, Satan-bashing comment like, "You couldn't live for God even when there was no devil to tempt you." He didn't say this. The way He handled temptation? Quoting Scripture.

You don't have to be amazing to defeat the enemy. Memorize! Put a Bible verse on your screensaver, put it on the background of your phone, put it on a note on your dashboard, or stick it on your fridge.

The devil will try to use your life purpose against you. If he cannot get you to reject God's call, he will distort it into a selfish thing. Jacob, an ancestor of the nation of Israel, knew he had a purpose to lead over his twin brother.[334] He tried to fulfill his life purpose in a selfish (devilish) way by manipulation and deceit.[335]

God favored the first man and woman, but they took the bait of Satan by grasping after equality with God.[336] Unlike those two, Jesus did not think of godhood as something up for grabs but humbled Himself instead.[337] He knew the path to the highest place in the universe was to humble Himself. No shortcuts.

A person cheating on a test is taking a shortcut not just around morals but around education. A cheating accounting student, for example, might graduate and get a job, but then have to Google information on how to file for an S-corporation. His

---

[333] Luke 4:12, LITV, from Deuteronomy 6:16.
[334] See Genesis 25:23-26.
[335] See Genesis 25:29-34 and 27:1-42.
[336] See Genesis 3:6.
[337] See Philippians 2:6-9.

shortcuts could blindside him to certain details which, when left out, cause him to be taken to court. A brain surgeon might take shortcuts to get through school, but he will have cheated himself and bring harm to his patients. If there is a path to be a neurosurgeon, there is a path to being a Christian—no shortcuts around God's plan.

Would it be wrong for Jesus to desire all the kingdoms of this world? Ruling over all nations is His purpose. Was it wrong for Abraham to want a child? Of course not. God intended him to have a son, but the path to that promise included his wife (doh!), not shacking up with the cleaning lady.[338] Abraham decided to take a shortcut around that detail and ended up with all kinds of problems.

Jacob also wanted a shortcut around God's plan—by manipulating to get his way instead of letting God work out the details. Eve and Adam (tempted in a garden, not the wilderness) took a shortcut around God's plan, sinking their teeth into the forbidden fruit. Each of us will have temptations to take shortcuts—to hurry God's plans for us.

This is the work of the devil: to get you to find the easy way around God's plan. Instead of following the Lord's Way, people look for shortcuts around it. A shortcut eliminates self-discipline and patience, driven by a desire to end up at the same destination. God's plans for us include the process, not just the result.

God wants us to prosper. He has provisions for how to bless us. Gambling away the rent money is not one of them. Taking loans we don't repay? Those are shortcuts. Always begging your boss to give you a raise? That is not the godly plan. Stealing is not either. How about hard work? Giving? Investing in others? These are God's paths to provision.

---

[338] Abraham had a child with his wife's helper named Hagar, but this was not the man God intended as the chosen offspring. This was a shortcut around God's plan of giving him a child through his wife.

181

What about love? Is there a God-plan? Yes. Anything else is of the devil. Pornography is a vile shortcut. So are other sexual experiences outside of God's foundation of marriage.

God not only has a destination, but He has a method to get there. God's Way brings Him glory. Jesus was baptized to fulfill all righteousness—to follow the full path, not find a way around it. Do we want Jesus's blessings, or do we want His Way? Why seek His truth and life without seeking His path?

What if quoting Scripture and resisting temptation was the Way to defeat the devil, for example? Are you using some other method? A shortcut? Or are you following the method of the Master? Will you keep trying to beat the enemy in your own strength or His?

After forty days of dwelling among wild beasts,[339] going without food, and dealing with Satan, Jesus sees this phase come to a close. The devil left Him alone until a good opportunity came up again.[340] After you resist and run the devil off, stay strong because he will come back later, like a rat trying to find a way in.

Meanwhile, the angels came and served Jesus's needs.[341] We first glimpsed angels at the Savior's birth, announcing the good news and singing His arrival. They appear this time next to the Man nearly starved to death out in the wild, it must have been quite a contrast.

Angels are both messengers and workers. Want angelic attention? Learn to use the Scriptures and resist temptation. God's warriors stand by His written orders.

---

[339] See Mark 1:13.
[340] See Luke 4:13.
[341] See Matthew 4:11.

THIS WAY, PLEASE

WHILE JESUS WAS GONE for over a month, what was John the Immerser doing? Washing and witnessing, preparing people for Jesus. It might have been a little awkward after baptizing Him and all. Where Jesus had gone after His big debut?

If John was to decrease in publicity while Jesus increased, why can the crowds only see John right now and not Jesus?

John: "I am here to show you the Lord!"

The crowd: "Where is He?"

John: ...

He continued witnessing, pointing others to Him. Witnessing is a good thing to do, right? Sometimes you hear a believer say something like: "I used to be a big, bad thug who beat up women and small children. Then, my life turned around. Now, I cook at the soup kitchen and give out toys at Christmas time." That almost sounds like a testimony for Jesus, except something important is missing: Jesus!

We do not testify how great we are because of God, but how great He is in spite of us. Tell people where you came from as long as they see Jesus in that story. Sometimes the sordid details of one's past life can cloud the account so much the listener cannot get over how "big and bad" the speaker was. Make sure you emphasize how "big and good" Jesus is.

John was the greatest of all prophets until his time, and he refused to block others' views of Jesus. Many scholars believe Mark wrote his Gospel first and that book places John as the opening event of the New Testament. The last prophecy in the last book of the Old Testament says an Elijah would come.[342] John the Immerser was the prophesied Elijah; God continued where He left off.

John came to bulldoze a path. Priests and Levites came out to challenge this man who had abandoned their clan. Even when all John could see was trees, hills, and valleys (obstacles and resistance), he kept building the highway, proclaiming the message of the Messiah.

The Temple workers had designated roles in worship to the Lord. They had an established program which was much bigger than a man standing in the river. Imagine the intimidating stares when they scowled at him and asked, "Who are you?"[343]

Power brokers do not like someone upsetting their equilibrium. Sometimes people who work for God begin to think they are God, as we see these leaders do. John knew his identity and was not looking for popularity or acceptance. He knew who he was and who he wasn't.

You will have people you look up to who may also grill you one day. They will raise an eyebrow and ask, "Who do you think you are?" John was not a rebel, out trying to do his own thing. That would raise my eyebrows, too. John was not arrogantly trying to build his own tribe. His confidence came from his calling.

---

[342] See Malachi 4:5; Mark 1:4.
[343] John 1:19, LITV.

They asked John if he was a reincarnated Elijah.[344] Nope. John was not going around as some do today, lying down on the grave of a spiritual person and asking for their power. He was not trying to take a big title or suck someone else's calling and labels for himself. Because of his humility, John would not boast of his role as the new Elijah.

In response to more questions, John told them upfront that he was not the Christ (Messiah) that Daniel had promised.[345] Was he the great Prophet that Moses said would come like himself?[346] Nope, not John. Jesus would fulfill both of those prophecies.

Knowing who he isn't, these religion pros then demand, "What do you say about yourself?"[347] Your connection with Jesus is not about you, but you had better know who you are. John learned his identity the same place you will find yours: "It is written!"[348] In Scripture, we not only see Jesus but begin to see ourselves in right perspective after we do.

John moved north to Bethabara to baptize.[349] This area of "beyond Jordan" was east of the Jordan River in a place also called Perea. Apparently, John has worked his way up the Jordan valley, baptizing converts in the river. Bethabara, (which means 'house of the ford') was located a day's journey from Galilee but a couple days' north of Jerusalem, so from its name and these

---

[344] See John 1:21.
[345] See John 1:20.
[346] See John 1:21 with Deuteronomy 18:15-18.
[347] John 1:22, LITV.
[348] See John 1:23.
[349] See John 1:28-29. Both John 1:26 and 29 indicate that Jesus had already been baptized at this point when John is defending Him and his role in presenting Him.

indicators, it must have been a large sandbar or ford in the river near the Sea of Galilee.[350]

John had not randomly happened to fulfill prophecy. He saw his place in the Scriptures and lived it. John persisted at doing what he was doing because he knew his purpose to prepare the Way of the Lord.

Not find a shortcut around the Lord.

Not find a popular program.

Not adopt a religious tradition.

If there is only one God, then there is only one Way. Today, most Christian religious people are not following the Way. Instead, they seek paths, shortcuts, around it. We will see exactly the Way better as we continue in this journey.

Some days are more exciting than others. The day John baptized Jesus was "off the charts." Now, John can't see Jesus anywhere, yet he stays on task telling others about Him.

Pharisees had influenced the hecklers from the Temple. Those purists believed that if they lived perfectionist lives, the Anointed would show up in their midst. The self-proclaimed religious experts try to make John feel small: "What are you baptizing for if you are not the Anointed One of Daniel, the prophet Elijah of old, or the Prophet Moses promised?"[351]

I remember overcoming the inertia to talk to a coworker about Jesus one day. I had no idea what I was doing, but my pastor had said to get people to attend Easter service. My coworker kind of groaned and said, "What, are you gonna be—a preacher or something?"

---

[350] See hints of this location in John 1:29, 35, 43; 10:40; 11:6, 39.
[351] See John 1:24-25.

Defensively I said, "No." The truth is I did not know who I was at that point.

To know who I am, I must know who Jesus is. John clarified that he had a role in the Jesus journals, but he pointed out that those religious experts were punching at a shadow. They needed to see the One among them.[352]

John has lost sight of Jesus but not his faith in Him.[353] He still "sees" Jesus in everything he does and says. Even when your senses do not respond, your faith keeps you focused on Him. Sometimes you cannot "feel" God, but He is still there, working a plan, including you in it.

---

[352] See John 1:26.
[353] See John 1:27.

LOOK AT HIM!

I HAVE GONE DOWN THE WRONG PATH. I'm not just talking about sin, because everyone has done that. In this race for righteousness, I have missed the path at times. I made the mistake of thinking I would win if I found more rules to keep and even made some of my own; at other times, I blundered by thinking I could just do as I pleased. We each have pathways of how we think about religious things.

The reason I have invited you for this immersion in the Gospels is so that we can take the time to make adjustments and get on the right road. Our minds develop highways: habitual ways of thinking. If you walk through the woods, you do not leave much of a mark. Walking that same path every day will wear down the grass and brush until a clear path emerges. Pathways in our minds become wider, deeper, more permanent until they are like paved highways. These pathways include emotional triggers, thought processes, and moral choices.

For example, a person who develops a pornography habit follows that mental (and spiritual and emotional) pathway so much that it becomes a rut or groove their mind goes to without effort. When the person realizes where such paths lead, he or she must repent—turn from that old path—and get on the high Way of the Lord. He always calls us to take the high road, not the shortcut.

Religious ruts can become train tracks. On such rigid rails, you do not turn a steering wheel to get off. Religiously ingrained folks have the hardest time turning toward the Messiah although their whole lives were steeped in rituals about Him.

Tears spring to my eyes as I think about all the people I have met like that today. They claim Jesus but do not know Him or follow Him. Like John, I want to point and yell, "Look!"

A day after those religious freight trains challenged John about his own identity, Jesus walks up again. John turns everyone's attention to Him: "Behold! The Lamb of God, taking away the sin of the world!"354 Basically, what his listeners heard was, "This man will die to take away the sins of all races and tribes." Lambs were to be sacrificed for each family, killed, bled, cooked, and eaten.355

Most Jews then did not celebrate a theology of salvation for non-Jews (they made Gentiles convert to Judaism and be circumcised). How would John know this kind of info about the Lamb being for all humanity? Isaiah. That prophet spoke of the One who would be led as a lamb to the slaughter and who would take on "our" punishment.356

John focused on informing everyone of Jesus's true identity. John confirms, "This is He about whom I said, 'After me comes a Man who has been before me, for He was preceding me.'"357 This One, born after John, came before him. John does not want us to glance, but to take a good, long look. We need to see more than what most people miss when they get a glimpse of this Man.

Someone might say John had a privilege we do not have. Since Mary and Elizabeth are relatives, some have said that John

---

354 John 1:29, LITV.
355 See Exodus 12:3-13.
356 Isaiah 53:7; Acts 8:32.
357 John 1:30, LITV.

and Jesus knew each other in younger years. John says something that helps us all not feel disqualified from this challenge to see Jesus: "I did not know Him."[358] For me, that debunks the myth that Jesus and John were buddies or close cousins.

Since John did not grow up with Jesus, His spiritual eyes had to be opened so he could "see" Jesus as we must. Jesus and John were not homies doing a ministry gig together—both grew up in different regions of Israel. John apparently had never seen Jesus until the day of His baptism.

Yet John "saw" Jesus. This helps me. I have never seen Jesus in the flesh. Like John, I can "see" Jesus without my natural eyes.

All John knew was that the Eternal One would be revealed to Israel, and so he said, "For this reason I came baptizing in water."[359] John knew he would see the Lord if he did what the Lord commanded. How did he know what the Lord required? By immersing himself in the Scriptures. By getting alone with the Lord in the wilderness.

John referred to the idea of Jesus being revealed. We call this revelation, "seeing Jesus." Jesus came to be shown or unveiled to the nation of Israel. But to see that reveal, you have to be looking. John grabs the religious people's attention and tells them, "Look! Just look!" If you think you are religiously correct, you quit looking. The smugness of being right blindfolds most Christians.

John's revelation of Jesus included things no one else had seen: He would be revealed while John immersed Him in water, the Spirit would appear as a dove coming to a permanent dwelling, and that this Man would be offspring of God.[360]

---

[358] John 1:31, LITV.
[359] John 1:31, LITV.
[360] See John 1:32-34.

Abraham climbed a mountain one day with his only beloved son[361] alongside him. The lad looked up at his dad and said, "Where is the lamb for our sacrifice?"

"My son," the old man replied while looking down at his promised son, "God will provide Himself... a lamb."[362]

When John looked at Jesus, he knew this was the Lamb who would die to save humanity. Someone might say, "John must have had special vision because I don't see stuff like that too well." You will see Jesus's closest followers struggle to see insights about Him even after following Him for years. Seeing Jesus is not an instantaneous thing—we must persist. The more we look, the more the fog lifts and the better we see Him.

John also "saw" that the One he immersed with water would also immerse others in Spirit. He saw that the fullness of the Spirit of God dwells in active force in this Man's body. John looked and saw that this not-so-ordinary Man would immerse others with that same Spirit.

---

[361] See Genesis 22:2 and Hebrews 11:17 calling Isaac the "only begotten."
[362] Genesis 22:7-8, NKJV.

DON'T JUST STARE

THE FOLLOWING DAY, John appears to have been conversing with his followers when Jesus walked up again. John announced: "Look at the Lamb of God!" The two turned and followed Jesus.[363]

We think of a lamb as a cute and cuddly pet. The Jews understood a male lamb to be doomed, especially in this context when John says He would take away sins. "Look!" he says in effect, "There's the Man intended to die for everyone."

Two people from the company of John's disciples heard his statement and noticed the Lord. Some people will never see Jesus until you point Him out to them. That's all it took for these two. They were ready!

These two men were John's disciples. The word "disciple" is not used at all in some Christian circles; in others, it has stretched out of shape. Let's be sure we are using the word biblically and not attaching assumed meanings to it.

"Disciple" is not a Christian-only word. Jewish rabbis had disciples. Rabbis were teachers who became so inspirational their followers wanted to embody what they taught and believed.

---

[363] See John 1:35-37.

"Rabbi" or "master" was not an official title or concrete role at that time other than that these men inspired and trained followers who then lived and taught those concepts to others. Many cultures have had gurus, mentors, consultants, and others who guided a "tribe" of followers.

Think for a moment of a college professor and students. While that situation is more formal, it is not far from the mark of a rabbi/disciple relationship. The teacher shapes the thinking of the students, and they must conform to the requirements and expectations to be included in the group. Disciples were not book-learning students, however. They were life-learning students.

For example, a rabbi had a haughty rich kid who expected special treatment. So, the rabbi told him to sit on the floor. The young man continued to sneer and put others down, so the rabbi told him to go sit outside by the beggar. The rich disciple quit that day, refusing the requirements of that apprenticeship. So, it was a voluntary role, but also a high honor to be accepted as a disciple of a certain man.

Most churches today focus on information transfer or emotional uplift rather than making disciples. The typical pastor speaks to large groups who sit and listen. Congregants find little room for interaction, personal coaching, accountability, or close friendship.

Should preachers speak to large groups of people? Yes, John did. However, we should not confuse that with discipleship. "Discipleship class" has become a catchword in churches that means "here we tell newcomers what we want them to do and not do" or "here's where you learn how this church is different from your last one." While good info might be given in such a class, that is not a picture of discipleship.

John's disciples learned his message and were developing into devotees who would live and teach John's concepts and principles (such as share what you have, do not demand higher

Daniel J. Koren

wages, and do not take advantage of others).[364] The two disciples who saw John point out Jesus then turned and followed Him. To follow a rabbi was to be his disciple, a big decision. John lost two disciples and Jesus gained them. "I must decrease, but He must increase."[365]

Ministers today must make the same decision as John: release their disciples to follow Jesus. I am sure most churches today would claim their purpose is to get people to follow Jesus, yet many have missed the concept. Many are making disciples of a denomination rather than of Jesus. If you criticize a person's denomination, some folks are so attached to it they will react as if to racial prejudice. We must decrease, but He must increase.

Like Luke, the first words that the Gospel of John recorded from Jesus are a question. He turns to the two tagging along behind Him and asks, "What do you seek?"[366] Asking questions is Jesus's way. He asked over three hundred questions that we have a record of.

Questions help us learn from people, rather than assume intentions. Disciples develop with question-asking. Jesus's questions helped them come to know themselves in light of God's plan. Were John's disciples following Him on a whim, a random impulse? They needed to think about what was drawing them to Him.

In response to Jesus's "How can I help you?" kind of question, the two followers acknowledge Him as "Teacher" or "Rabbi." They knew He was a leader who trained others in how to live.

The respectful title "rabbi" applied to those who taught *Torah*, the writings of Moses. Many rabbis developed their own codes of conduct, providing many different schools of thought

---

[364] See Luke 3:11-14.
[365] See John 3:30.
[366] John 1:38, LITV.

that various Jews would follow. Rather than an information-only teacher, think of a rabbi as a personal trainer. He would not only instruct but also observe and give points for improvement.

"Rabbi,... where do You stay?"[367] Asking Jesus where He lived was to invite themselves to learn from Him. Would this Rabbi allow them to be His disciples? Jesus said, "Come and see."[368] Each of us begins here.

If people will not come to Jesus, they cannot be His disciple. If they cannot "see" Him, they cannot be a disciple. It takes both closeness and awareness to belong to Jesus and later represent Him.

Jesus and His new followers arrived around four in the afternoon and it would be dark soon.[369] Since robbers lurked after dark, they probably spent the night at His house, too. They went to His home; this is how close disciples and rabbis became. To follow Jesus is to integrate our lives into His.

We now meet some of the key players in the Gospel chronicles. Andrew was one of the first two who followed Jesus.[370] Liking what he saw, Andrew does what disciples do: finds someone else to tell about Jesus. Traditional churches often try to get members to witness to others; a disciple does this naturally, and we will learn why later.

Andrew realized Jesus was the "Messiah,"[371] a word meaning 'the Anointed One.' This term was used for kings to whom special oil was ritually applied by pouring it onto their heads in dedication to the Lord. The Greek equivalent of that word forms our word "Christ" in the New Testament, also

---

[367] John 1:38, LITV.
[368] See John 1:39.
[369] See John 1:39.
[370] See John 1:40. Since the other disciple is not named, it is possible that this was John, author of the Gospel. He never drew attention to himself in his work.
[371] John 1:41.

meaning 'The Anointed.' We will see the impact of Jesus being the "Anointed One" in the sequel to this book.

In his excitement, Andrew brought on one of the heaviest hitters in the Jesus-narrative: Simon. Jesus redefines unstable Simon as the "Rock" and then proceeds to shape him into a massively influential man.[372] The words "Cephas" and "Peter" both mean 'stone' or 'rock.' I wonder if Jesus would have called him Rocky if He spoke English. This man's first glimpse of Jesus leaves him wide-eyed. How did Jesus know him and his dad? Who did He think He was to rename him? When you see Jesus, He will redefine you.

Andrew's biggest investment in the kingdom was inviting his brother to meet the Anointed for himself. He said what any disciple can say: "Come and see."

I once invited a man to church services saying, "We would love for you to join us." He said, "I won't join, but I might visit." He was being humorous of course, but this reminds me of how we often ask for a commitment from people who are not yet sure of what all is involved.

"Come and see" is an invitation to observation: "Try before you buy." If a person is not interested in at least considering Jesus, forcing them to commit will not help. Jesus will require things of His followers, but first, they must see who and what it is they are committing to.

---

[372] See John 1:42.

HE SEES THROUGH ME

APPRENTICES AGREE TO BE TRAINED for a purpose and a life-long skill. They understand the process will cost them. They know they will have to learn new habits and ways of thinking. They follow a master craftsman so they can become experts one day. A disciple is a protégé, an understudy, an apprentice.

Andrew, Peter, John, and others traveled at least a whole day away from home to be in this place where John was dunking people. To be "disciples of John," they had invested a lot of time learning from him. They were not just listeners among the crowds. They left comfort and tradition because they saw something better.

Everyone is a disciple of something or someone. Before we become committed to any cause, we need to be sure it is worth our total focus. These individuals demonstrate their radical willingness to follow Jesus.

Jesus then left Bethabara, where John was baptizing and went to Galilee. Heading toward home (Nazareth is in Galilee), Jesus tells Philip, "Follow Me."[373] Protégés of Jesus follow Him.

---

[373] John 1:43.

They don't just know about Him and collect books about Him—they know Him closely and imitate all He does.

Many people might have told Jesus, "Sure, I think the same way as you. I believe like you." People you meet will want to make Jesus all about an ideology, not a person or a friend. Such people are not ready to follow the person of Jesus. Discipleship is more than a philosophy or education.

Have you ever followed a recipe you found online only to have it come out all wrong? Sometimes reading the information or even watching someone else is not enough. Complicated things take not only info but coaching. Sometimes your timing needs to change, or the temperature, or the sequence of adding spice, salt, or sauce. You can read a book or watch a video on lifting weights, but you progress much better having an expert guide and correct you.

Would you rather buy a gym membership or hire a health coach? In a perfect world we would learn everything we need from a book, but not in Jesus's. He did not leave us just a Book—He included a coaching service, too. He gives more than information—He personally trains us if we will follow Him. Yes, right now, right where you are, He will teach you, observe your efforts, and guide you to fulfillment. We will learn together how to hear the Coach better.

I am not your coach, He is. My job is to help point out blindfolds that keep you from seeing your Coach. This book series, the handbooks, and accompanying resources are the gym where you can work out.

Philip[374] did not waste any time doing as was done to him: offering an invitation to follow Jesus. Either on the way or once

---

[374] He probably first met Jesus through Andrew and Peter, being that they were from the same hometown (John 1:44), they knew one another.

they got home, he found his buddy Nathaniel and told him they had found the Man—not just a message. This "telling others" thing is neither hard nor complicated.

If you are a deer hunter or avid nature watcher, imagine seeing a monster buck. If you get excited about seeing a buck in your backyard and want to tell someone else, you understand what it is like to say "Come and see!" Does Jesus excite you like that? Too many people hesitate to talk about Jesus because they think they have to have theological debates or get into arguments about politics or social issues if they bring Him up.

Old Nate has an instant objection for his joyous pal Phil. Philip explained, "We have found the One of whom Moses wrote in the Law and the Prophets, Jesus the son of Joseph, from Nazareth."[375]

Nate challenges his biblical interpretation: "Can any good thing be out of Nazareth?"[376] We aren't saying anyone was prejudiced here, but someone didn't think anything good could come out of the ghetto. Nathaniel probably only knew the Messiah would come from Bethlehem and hadn't caught the rest of the story.

Philip chose not to get into a debate with his friend. He simply offered the challenge each of us can give: "Come and see!"[377]

His man Nate did go and see. Jesus speaks to Him formative words as He did with Simon the Rock. "Behold, truly an Israelite in whom is no guile!"[378] A true Israelite would be one with the faith of Abraham and not having guile would mean he did not use deception but was honest. Jesus saw the best in this

---

[375] John 1:45, LITV.
[376] John 1:45, LITV.
[377] John 1:46.
[378] John 1:47, LITV.

friend of Philip's. Seeing Jesus will help us see ourselves better, too.

Nathan is shocked. He's never seen or heard of Jesus before, but this Man knows him. How does He know him? Jesus explains that He knew the man before Philip called him from under the fig tree, where he likely was cooling off from the heat of the day.[379] Jesus's statement that He knew the man before He saw him inspires Nate. He reacts, "Rabbi, You are the Son of God; You are the King of Israel."[380] These are heavy insights for a person who just started looking at Jesus!

Nathaniel now sees. Jesus works on a different level than an ordinary human would. His prophetic insight triggers an opening of Nate's eyes. Not only does he see more than the average person sees about this Man, but Nate also wants to see even more. Being an understudy of Jesus is a supernatural exercise. We learn to see and hear what is just out of reach of those who do not believe.

What Jesus does here in reaching Nate is not something you or I could learn from a book. For Jesus, this is natural. For us, this is the empowerment of the Spirit we call the Word of Knowledge. Jesus is able to speak to specific things in Ol' Nate's life by supernatural ability. Nate sees Him as King of Israel. There is more, though; He is King of much more than that. Disciples have their eyes opened to His uniqueness.

Jesus tells him, "You will see greater things than these."[381] There is always more to see. Some see faster than others, but we must all see Him. Your "big moments" with Jesus will keep getting bigger the longer you know Him.

Are you ready to see greater things than you have ever seen in your spiritual life? Are you ready to stretch beyond the

---

[379] See John 1:48.
[380] John 1:49, LITV.
[381] John 1:50, LITV.

greatest religious experiences you have ever had? You will see greater things on this journey!

Don't miss how Nate's eyes opened. First, Philip made himself vulnerable enough to talk to a skeptical friend and say, "Come and see." Who is the Lord leading you to invite with a come-and-see statement? How can that man or woman already see Jesus in your life?

Using the icon of Jacob's ladder, Jesus hints toward the deeper revelation Nate will receive. Jacob (also named Israel) had a dream while running from his twin who wanted to kill him. In this dream, angels climbed up from earth to the sky (the unseen realm) and back down again. Jacob named that place "Bethel" which means 'House of God.' Every Jew knew that.

Jesus told him, "From now on you will see Heaven opened, and 'the angels of God ascending and descending' on the Son of Man."[382] This makes His humanity the "House of God" where the angels come and go—He is the commander of Heaven's forces! The eternal God dwells in this house of flesh and bone. To make a long story short, old Nate will one day see Jesus as the fullness of God in the flesh, but for now, "King of Israel" is a good start.

To you, also, Jesus is saying, "You haven't seen anything yet!"

In the next book, we will see how Jesus begins to open the eyes of His followers. He will also begin training us how to talk to others about Him without creating a fight! Then, we will look deep into how He did what He did and how He can do those powerful things through us. Finally, we will see how none of us have any viable excuses when we see the kind of people Jesus

---

[382] John 1:51, LITV, quoting from Genesis 28:12.

welcomed and how He transformed them. See you in the next book as we do a spiritual *Factory Reset*!

APPENDIX A

"Opening Word"

"**I**N THE BEGINNING was the Word, and the Word was with God, and the Word was God." (John 1:1, NKJV)

As we examine the Gospel writings, we will tread carefully not to imprint our own ideas onto them. For example, there are many modern statements and Christianized arguments about the Gospel of John's early pics here. I won't dig through the filter drawer, but so many theological arguments color these verses in modern minds, and the assumptions are layered deeply. Some of those agendas distort the masterpiece and insult the artist.

We are not here to tell John what we think we see or to push onto his work what we think we understand about Jesus. John was there. We are going to listen to the man who not only saw Jesus with physical eyes but saw through spiritual eyes who He really was.

To understand this passage best, let's agree to seek to know what the original viewers would have gotten from this work. That will help us better understand what we should get from these passages, too. So far, John has not used the name

"Jesus." His name does not appear until John's seventeenth frame (chapter 1, verse 17). And don't worry, it is all leading up to Him, but the way John has laid out this display to focus on Jesus is strategic, and we don't want to get ahead of that.

The Jews of that day would not have been shocked at John's "Word" being from the beginning. They knew that "Through the Word of Jehovah the heavens were made; and all their host were made by the breath of His mouth."[383] They often used "Word" as a name for God.[384] When John, a Jew himself, shows the Word was God, his Jewish viewers leaned forward in their seats. What God spoke was His very desires—the very essence of who He is.

The non-Jewish audience (people the Jews called "Gentiles") surely had a little reaction to this first snap from John. This glimpse of the Word was not just a lucky shot. John was inspired to take some time and set up this frame to capture a wide-angle view that both Jews and non-Jews would have to examine closely.

The Greeks taught about a being or entity called *Logos*.[385] John's Gospel is written in Greek (from that we get our English versions). Although there were other words John could have used, the Spirit led him to choose a loaded one.

---

[383] Psalm 33:6, LITV. The Greek *Septuagint* translated this "Word" with *Logos* (Psalm 32:6, LXX), giving precedent for the personification of *Logos* in John 1:1.

[384] The *Targums*, a type of Jewish commentary, referenced the Creator as Word of the Lord. The Hebrew for this "Word" is *memra*. See Craig Keener, *The Gospel of John: a commentary*, Vol. 1, (Grand Rapids, MI: Hendrickson, 2003), 341-50. There were other substitution words for God, such as *Hashem*, "The Name," since they did not want to say His sacred name.

[385] The name given to the divine mind in Platonic and Stoic thinking. For Philo, who spoke from a Jewish background while embracing some Greek philosophies, the *Logos* was the agent of creation (in a very simplified summary).

At first, the Greek readers of this Gospel would probably have been nodding their heads in agreement because their *Logos* character was part of the pipeline for the creation of the physical world and considered by some to be the agent involved in the making of it. There is much we could say here about Philo and middle-Platonic thought, but we will do so in a later book.[386]

The Gospel then grabbed the Jews' attention with this next phrase: The *Logos* was God. If the Jews are on the edge of their seats, the Greeks have dropped back in theirs, not having expected this development. Jews thought of God's spoken word as an attribute of Himself. Greeks did not say it this way. God was His own agent in creation? Absurd!

Just in case they didn't catch the full view with the first snapshots, one more pic: "The same was in the beginning with God."[387] Since the creative Word comes from God we will not find it absent from Him or Him from it.

If any of the onlookers were daydreaming, John takes a panoramic shot showing that this is about Creation in the Beginning: "All things came into being through" the Word. Without the Word, "not even one thing came into being that has come into being."[388] Everything that exists was made by the Word of the Lord.

The Jews have found their faith confirmed (so far) and the Greeks just learned something new. The "Word" was, in fact, the mighty God. Now, they all know this story is going to be good.

---

[386] We cannot say for sure that John meant to tie this "Word" to contemporary Hellenistic thinking, Philo, protognosticism, or Targumic expressions, but those all come into view with the language used. This is not to say John was a deep theologian orchestrating this complex statement. The Spirit guided what he wrote. In spite of the history behind the use of "Word," none of those competing ideologies crowd into the spotlight. Letting us know that what God was the Word was, the text clearly put all those old views out of the picture or redefined them.

[387] John 1:2, KJV.

[388] John 1:3, LITV.

Even better when John says, "The Word became flesh." Now both the Jews and Greeks are out of their seats, not expecting this plot twist.

From the beginning, we see the Scriptures working to remove blindfolds. Looking too closely at a couple of words like this has caused some theologians to miss John's epic metaphor. John chapter 1 recasts the story of Creation to show us Jesus in His proper light. We have addressed some of these things here to keep pace with the Gospel order, however, the details of these truths will be fleshed out later in the Gospels, and we will take a longer look in a future book.

Appendix B

"Say the Name"

T HE REASON FOR SO MANY OPTIONS is partially due to the nature of any language to change over the years. For example, read about the "great vowel shift" that occurred in England near the end of the middle ages and how our letter "a" went from the sound of "ah" in "father" to the now typical "a" in "apple." Different regions of the world can alter a language such as the difference between the Spanish used in Spain and what is spoken in Mexico.

The Hebrew language died for a time and exact sounds were lost through years of disuse. Modern Hebrew has borrowed sounds from Spanish and German. No one can pronounce any Hebrew word with total surety that it matches what was said millennia ago. Written Hebrew now has vowel points which are little marks and dots beneath, beside, or above the consonants.

Even ancient Hebrew had its own variations. Let's assume the name "Yeshua" was the proper name for Jesus in Hebrew. Some Hebrew speakers did not pronounce the "sh" in the Hebrew letters and only said the "s." This is the origin of the legendary term "shibboleth" where several thousands of those from the tribe of Ephraim were killed because their pronunciation betrayed them to the enemy.[389]

The Hebrew letter for "sh" appears in the middle of the word *Yeshua*. Mary and Joseph came from different regions of Israel. She from the north and he the south. They might have both pronounced the Child's name differently. Joseph would have pronounced it something like "Yeshua." Mary, influenced by Ephraim in the north, might have said it more like "Yesua." I am not at all trying to prove the parents said the name differently but make a point that the exact pronunciation could have varied while He was alive.

The New Testament came to us in Greek with His name as *Iesous* ("Ee-ey-soos"). Every verse we quote about the Name of Jesus was not written in Hebrew but in a Greek transliteration of that name. Paul preached to the Gentiles of *Iesous*, not *Yeshua*. Jesus is never directly referred to in the Bible with a Hebrew word. Those people, who temporarily convinced me many years ago that the Apostles used the name of Yeshua, have no written, biblical evidence of Jesus's name in Hebrew.

Latin became a major player on the world scene in the centuries after Christ. From the Greek *Iesous* came the Latin *Iesus*. Later, this Name came to English as "Jesus." Again, notice the differences in initial letters.

It is hard to determine conclusively how the Hebrew letter was pronounced back in that time. In modern Hebrew, it is a "y" sound. At one time it was the "j" sound. A contemporary illustration of the use of "y" and "j" sounds can be found in the Spanish language. Some of my Spanish-speaking friends articulate the "y" and "ll" sounds differently. (The Spanish *ll*, double letter "l," makes the sound of "y.") Those who follow the older Castilian influence pronounce this letter as a "j" sound, but the more typical use is the "y" sound. For example, a simple

---

[389] See Judges 12:5-6. Thanks to my friend Jason Weatherly for pointing this out.

Spanish phrase which most would pronounce as "Yo estoy," others will pronounce as "Jo estoy."

If you pronounce "j" and then "y" you will notice the physical similarity between how both sounds are performed. The "j" is simply a "y" sound overlaid with a "z" or "zh" sound. Ancient Italian inscriptions have the name of Jesus as *Gesú* or something similar which shows that the soft-G sound (same as the "j") goes back many centuries and English is not the only language to use it for the Savior's name.[390] I am no linguistic expert, but I believe if we could trace back the changes in Hebrew pronunciations we would find that as new languages incorporated Hebrew words, they simply took a snapshot of how it was pronounced in that era.

How can any of us, who have not lived a mere 200 years, claim to know how people pronounced the Lord's name 2,000 years ago? We cannot, and the precise enunciation of the Name is not the point. Would the Lord reject people with a speech impediment or thick accent? It would be superstitious to assume that the Name only works if we say it with the right intonation, accent, and guttural vibrations.

We must know Jesus as the God-who-saves (Yahweh-Savior). Seeing Jesus (not just saying) is our goal. In a later book, we will see the power of speaking His name for those who see and know Him in truth.

---

[390] Gerhard Kittel and Gerhard Friedrich, *Theological Dictionary of the New Testament*, Vol. 2, (Grand Rapids, MI: Eerdmans, 1965), 286.

Daniel J. Koren

BIBLIOGRAPHY

Beasley-Murray, George R. *John*. 2nd ed. Word Biblical Commentary 36. Nashville: Nelson, 1999.

Bock, Darrell. *Luke*. Vol 1. Baker Exegetical Commentary on the New Testament. Grand Rapids, Mich.: Baker Academic, 1994.

_____. *Luke*. NIV Application Commentary. Grand Rapids, Mich.: Zondervan, 1996.

Burge, Gary M. *John*. NIV Application Commentary. Grand Rapids, Mich.: Zondervan, 2000.

France, R. T. *The Gospel of Matthew*. New International Commentary on the New Testament. Grand Rapids, Mich.: Eerdmans, 2007.

Keener, Craig. *The Gospel of John*. Peabody, Mass.: Hendrickson, 2003.

_____. *The Gospel of Matthew: A Social-Rhetorical Commentary*. Grand Rapids, Mich.: Eerdmans, 2009.

Kittel, Gerhard, and Gerhard Friedrich, *Theological Dictionary of the New Testament*, Vol. 2, Grand Rapids, MI: Eerdmans, 1965.

Norris, David. *I AM*. WAP Academic, 2009.

Wilkins, Michael J. *Matthew*. NIV Application Commentary. Grand Rapids, Mich.: Zondervan, 2004.

ABOUT THE AUTHOR

DANIEL J. KOREN has written for a variety of magazines, teaching curriculums, and other resources focused on helping people in biblical understanding and personal growth. With over one million words in print, Daniel's new goal is to give away over a million ebooks and help as many people as possible. Currently, he has focused his time and efforts on helping believers have a clear understanding of the Kingdom of God. This includes books, study guides, and teaching tools covering every verse of the New Testament. In his free time, Daniel enjoys reading (and smelling the aroma of) thick reference books, traveling with his wife Leanne (who often drives their motorhome so he can write), and hanging out with their eight children who provide so much inspiration and motivation for what he does.

ADVENTURE AWAITS

YOU HAVE MERELY SCRATCHED the surface on the Jesus story. This book introduced the topic and the second book, *Factory Reset*, launches into the action, mystery and wonder of the events of Jesus's life. Now that your attention is focused on the right Person, see what He says, how He reacts, and what He teaches.

In the next volume, watch Jesus:

- welcome and transform tough-to-love people
- open the eyes of His followers.
- train us how to talk to others about Him
- show how He can do powerful things through us.

See you in the next book of the Jesus in 20/20 series!

www.ingramcontent.com/pod-product-compliance
Lightning Source LLC
Chambersburg PA
CBHW061258110426
42742CB00012BA/1968